JOE WICKS

PROTEIN

in 15

JOE WICKS
PROTEIN
in 15

Easy, tasty, unprocessed
meals for everyone

LEAP

Contents

Introduction

Welcome to *Protein in 15*. I'm so excited to share this new collection of delicious recipes with you.

This book is all about fast food made healthy, with an emphasis on protein. Protein is an essential part of a balanced diet and is crucial for supporting health and fitness, and there are so many benefits to a diet high in protein.

Including whole-food sources of protein in balanced meals can help you feel fuller for longer and stabilise blood glucose levels. When these levels are stabilised, you get fewer cravings, which helps you to be more mindful when it comes to swerving sugary 'treats' and ultra-processed foods (UPFs). The potential satiating effect of increased protein intake may also naturally lead to you consuming less food.

The main aim of this book is simple: to help you and your family eat better more often, and to ultimately avoid UPFs as much as possible. If you can successfully do this, it can be life-changing for you in so many ways.

I went on a personal journey with this stuff while filming a documentary for Channel 4 that explored UPFs. It was eye-opening to see and be able to fully understand the ingredients that go into our food, especially food made in a factory with lots of ingredients and with a long shelf life. To be honest, most of these types of food aren't real food. Dr Chris van Tulleken describes UPFs as 'industrially produced edible substances', which kind of makes sense when you realise that most of the ingredients are chemicals and not real food at all. It is such a huge and complex problem, but rather than focusing on the problem, I want to focus on the solution. The solution is making more meals from scratch, using whole ingredients. If we all do this, we stand a better chance of navigating the crazy food environment we currently live in. Until we see big changes in the behaviour of food companies, changes in government legislation and changes in the marketing of UPFs, which targets us daily, I believe we have to regain some power over our own diets. When you cook more, you have more control over what you eat and you can take care of yourself. I have seen this transform so many people's lives for the better: when I support people to eat less processed food, they often mention that they have more energy, and have fewer digestive issues, too.

The recipes in this book are suitable for everyone, regardless of age or fitness level, so whether you're trying to build muscle in the gym or going through the menopause, I hope these recipes inspire and motivate you to step into the kitchen. All I really want is for more people to feel better more often, and I'm confident that if you give some of these recipes a go, you'll start to feel great and want to continue with the lifestyle.

I know there are hundreds of new cookery books to choose from each year, so thank you for giving my recipes a chance. I appreciate the support. If you would like more recipe ideas, check out my Instagram @thebodycoach.

Thank you, Joe x

About the recipes

The recipes in this book are broken into six chapters: Joe's Home 'Takeaways', Easy Peasy Dinners, Pasta & Noodle Winners, Veg & Plant-powered, Lunchbox Inspo and Fast-prep, Slow-cook Bangers.

My aim with cooking has always been to make recipes that are quick to cook or quick to prep. There are some longer slow-cooked recipes in here too, but I think you'll be really happy with the variety. When you get started, it may feel like you are buying lots of new spices, nuts, seeds and herbs, but once you have them, you'll notice they appear in lots of the recipes so they will all get used up eventually.

Remember, any of these meals can be eaten at any time, so if you fancy a stir-fry for breakfast or overnight oats for dinner, that's all fine. You do you, and eat what feels right for you.

The key to long-term success and getting the most out of this book is to plan your meals into the week ahead and get into batch cooking. This saves money, saves time, and really helps you stay on track.

Recipe symbols

Gluten-free	Vegetarian	Freezable	Vegan

Why is protein important?

Protein is an essential macronutrient made up of amino acids. The amino acid molecules form the building blocks of protein: there are 21 in total and 9 of these are essential. These essential ones can't be made in the body and must be consumed in our diet. Most animal protein sources contain all essential amino acids; plant-based eaters need to make sure they include a variety of plant-based protein sources (see page 16) throughout the day.

Protein contributes to a wide variety of functions that keep our body healthy; many things, from the composition of our hormones to our DNA, are related to protein. Our protein needs are individual, and vary throughout our life as our bodies grow and change.

Protein is often described as the main building block of muscle. This is true – protein is essential for building and repairing muscle tissue – but the role and function of protein in the body goes way further than this. Some benefits and functions might be obvious, but others may come as a surprise. The following list of benefits emphasises just how important protein is for us all, regardless of our age or gender, when it is included as part of a balanced and varied diet and healthy lifestyle.

HEALTH BENEFITS

Builds and Maintains Muscle Mass

- Protein contains essential amino acids needed to build and repair muscle. This is especially important for athletes and ageing adults. It also has a proven role in growth, not just in childhood and adolescence, but also in pregnancy.

May Support Weight Loss and Fat Loss

- Eating balanced meals containing a good portion of protein helps us to feel fuller for longer. It helps slow the rate at which our food is digested and absorbed, which can mean we feel less hungry and may consume less throughout the day.

Boosts your Digestion

- This effect is called the higher thermic effect of food (TEF): your body requires more energy to digest and absorb protein than other macronutrients such as carbohydrates and fat.

Supports Recovery from Injury

- Eating protein as part of a balanced diet and lifestyle is an important component in supporting tissues to repair, which is essential for wound healing and post-surgery recovery.

Helps Maintain Healthy Bones

- Varied high-protein diets, especially those rich in dairy, fish and legumes, support an improved bone mineral density, which can help reduce the risk of fractures, particularly as we age (alongside other important nutrients such as calcium and vitamin D).

May Improve Hair, Skin and Nails

- Keratin, collagen and elastin are all protein-based structures, and adequate intake of protein supports their growth and repair.

May Help Support Stable Blood Glucose Levels

- Protein takes longer to be digested and absorbed than carbohydrates and fats. Consuming it with carbohydrates can slow the rate that glucose is released from the stomach into the small intestine and lead to a slower rise in blood glucose levels. Fibre and fat have a similar impact, so consume protein as part of a balanced meal that contains healthy fats, fibre and high-fibre wholegrains where possible.

Supports Strong Immune Function

- Antibodies, immune cells and enzymes are made of proteins, which are essential for immune defence (when consumed as part of a healthy diet).

Can Help Preserve Lean Muscle as We Age

- An adequate protein intake alongside a balanced diet may help to reduce the risk of age-related muscle loss, potentially helping to improve strength and mobility.

May Help Reduce Visceral Abdominal Fat

- Some research has shown that higher protein diets may help to reduce the metabolically active fat, known as visceral fat, that is deposited around the abdomen. This type of fat is associated with increased risk of diseases such as cardiovascular disease and type 2 diabetes.

Supports Physical Performance

- Alongside other important nutrients such as carbohydrates, protein has an important role in terms of physical performance and recovery. helping our muscles function at their best.

Supports Hormone Balance

- Many hormones (like insulin, growth hormones and glucagon) are protein-derived or regulated by amino acid availability. Protein intake helps support a wide variety of the body's regulatory and hormonal systems.

. . . .

As you can see, there are so many benefits to having a protein-rich diet. It really is an essential part of daily life for good health and happiness.

. . . .

Why I love whole-food protein

I am particularly interested in the link between food and our gut–brain connection, and the impact this has on mood and mental health. I notice an almost instant negative effect on my mood when I consume lots of sugar and UPFs. I just get down and feel flat for the rest of the day. To say it simply: good food, good mood, junk food, junk mood.

This is why I've written this book and focussed on unprocessed, high-protein recipes. Whole foods tend to be richer in many nutrients and higher in fibre than processed ones, meaning it tends to take your body more time and energy to absorb the nutrients they contain. When my meals are fuelled by whole-food sources of protein, I feel fuller for longer, my blood glucose levels are stabilised and I crave sugar a lot less. This means I eat fewer calories over a week and naturally – as a by-product – this can lead to losing body fat and staying lean all year round.

Protein has been a buzzword for many years in the health and fitness world, and I am sure you have heard lots about the link between protein and building muscle. You will have noticed also the explosion of a whole new category of food products wearing the proud badge 'added protein', a health claim marked on food items such as processed yoghurt, breads, crisps, snack bars, shakes and even ice creams, but don't be fooled. I have discovered that many of these UPF products are made with a whole concoction of stuff we really don't want or need in our bodies. It's so important to read the ingredient lists – on closer inspection, you'll often see a long list of additives, sweeteners, emulsifiers and stabilisers, which are added so that the product is cheaper to make and keeps for longer. Many of the ingredients and additives have harmful effects on our short- and long-term health, and the way these ingredients are listed on labels can be misleading and difficult to understand.

Sugar is not actually a reward or a treat. That's the story sold to us by the food companies that are trying to sell us their sugary products. Start seeing healthy food as the treat and protein as the reward.

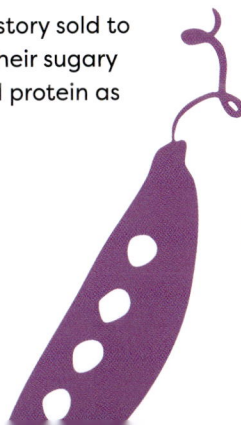

Who needs protein?

Unlike fat and carbohydrates, we don't store protein in our body, so regular consumption is important. Although our individual nutritional requirements are unique, and change throughout our lifetime, we all need to think about protein. It's not just something that's required by keen gym-goers looking to get bigger arms, it is a non-negotiable for all of us, regardless of age, gender or fitness level.

Everyone (Baseline Need)

• Protein is essential for muscle maintenance, supporting healthy immune function and bone growth and health.

• Even sedentary people need protein to maintain basic bodily functions.

Children and Teenagers

• Children and adolescents grow rapidly, and protein is critical for developing healthy, strong muscles, bones and organs.

Athletes and Active People

• Exercise increases protein needs for muscle repair, growth and recovery.

• Endurance and strength athletes require more protein than sedentary people.

People Trying to Lose Weight

• Protein helps increase satiety, which can lessen cravings and help preserve lean muscle mass when you are trying to lose fat.

Older Adults (50+)

• Helps prevent muscle loss (sarcopenia) and maintain strength, mobility and bone health.

I am not medically trained, or a registered dietitian, though I've consulted an expert dietitian throughout writing this book. If you have any medical concerns, you should always see a doctor, and if you require individual dietary support, consult a registered dietitian.

Pregnant and Breastfeeding Women

• When consumed as part of a healthy diet and lifestyle, protein supports the growth of the baby's tissues, brain and organs in the womb, and helps maintain the mother's body tissue and milk supply.

People Recovering from Illness or Surgery

• Protein helps support tissue repair, wound healing, and immune system strength during recovery.

Vegetarians and Vegans

• Complete proteins (containing all essential amino acids) are especially important for vegetarians and vegans, as plant sources can contain lower levels of some amino acids. Consume a wide variety of plant sources of protein regularly to meet your body's essential amino acid requirements.

People with Certain Medical Conditions

• Cancer patients, people with burns or trauma, and some people with chronic illnesses often need to increase their protein intake for healing and immune support.

Who Might Need to be Cautious

• *People with kidney disease (especially advanced stages) may need to moderate their protein intake, under medical supervision.*

• *Consuming very high quantities of protein (especially from supplements or poor-quality sources) isn't recommended for most people.*

Sources of whole-food protein

Protein can be found in many foods, including lots of ultra-processed foods, but not all sources of protein are equal. Real food is the best source of protein.

Some foods are described as 'complete proteins' because they contain all of the essential amino acids needed by the body. Others are described as 'incomplete proteins' – with these proteins, it's important to combine several other sources of protein throughout the week to ensure you are consuming all of the essential amino acids. Try not to overthink this, just aim to include a variety of protein sources in your meals, for example: eggs, salmon, chicken, chickpeas and quinoa. This will ensure you cover all bases.

While there is nothing wrong with having the occasional whey protein shake after a workout, don't rely on it for protein consumption. Supplements should supplement a good diet and not replace real food. Put simply, real food wins over dust. I've listed all of the different categories and types of protein on pages 15–16 to help you with meal planning and remind you which wonderful whole foods are naturally rich in protein.

Don't feel pressured into eating only animal protein every day, or eating only plant-based sources every day – this book is about cooking real food that you love and enjoy, and eating intuitively, so pick and choose what works for you and your family. Some days I eat a fully plant-based diet, some days I eat animal protein at every meal, and other days I fast. The most important thing to consider is your own energy levels, your own mood and your own lifestyle. 'Eat to feel awesome' is a simple concept I like to promote. If you feel awesome eating steak, egg and avocado every morning, then that's it for you (though it's worth bearing in mind that current NHS guidelines recommend not eating red meat more than once a week). If you feel better when you eat oats with chia seeds, nuts and berries for breakfast, then that's the one for you.

What's important for overall gut health and wellness is to have as much variety in your week as possible with the food you consume, so be brave: every now and again try something totally new from this book and challenge yourself.

Meals not snacks

You'll notice I haven't included a chapter on snacks or breakfasts. I have in some of my previous books, but in this book I wanted to focus on main meals.

You're probably thinking, 'Oh Joe! I love snacks and I wanted some sweet treat ideas!' Here is the truth, though... I think snacking is our biggest downfall from a health point of view. It's not our fault: the food industry has tricked us all into thinking we need to be snacking in between every meal. This conditioning happens from a very young age and is fully normalised by the time we are toddlers. Think about what's on the shelves in supermarkets, petrol stations and even airports. It's pretty much all UPFs. The snackification of food has become even more apparent in recent years, and most of these 'convenient' products are targeted at our children, and most recently many have 'added protein' claims. Arghhhhh... I can feel myself getting angry.

Animal-based protein sources

Meat & Poultry	Fish & Seafood	Eggs & Dairy
Chicken breast/thigh	Salmon	Whole eggs
Turkey breast	Tuna (fresh or tinned)	Egg whites
Lean beef (sirloin, mince)	Cod	Greek yoghurt
Lamb (lean cuts)	Haddock	Cottage cheese
Pork loin, tenderloin	Mackerel	Hard cheeses (cheddar, Parmesan)
Game meats (venison, duck)	Sardines	Ricotta
	Prawns/shrimp	Milk (whole, semi-skimmed)
	Crab/lobster	Kefir
	Anchovies	Quark
	Trout	

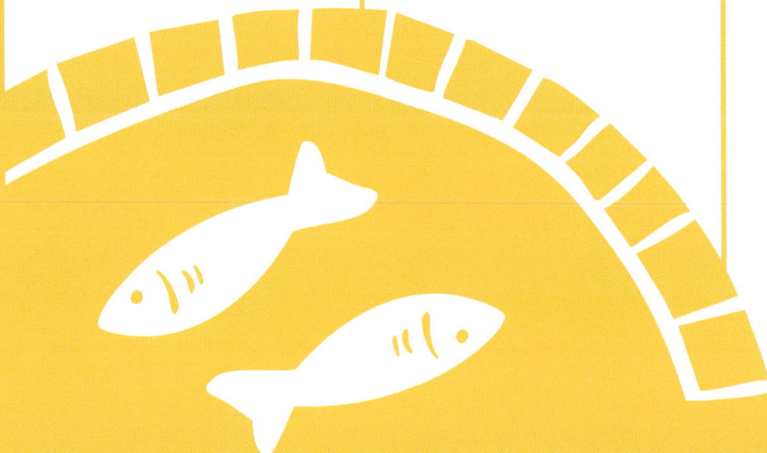

Plant-based sources

(Some are complete, others can be combined for a full amino-acid profile)

Legumes	Soy Products	Grains	Nuts & Seeds
Lentils (red, green, brown)	Tofu (firm, silken)	Quinoa (complete protein)	Almonds
Chickpeas	Tempeh	Brown rice	Walnuts
Black beans	Soy milk (fortified)	Buckwheat	Cashew nuts
Kidney beans	Soy yoghurt	Amaranth	Pistachios
Pinto beans		Oats	Peanuts
Navy beans		Barley	Chia seeds
Cannellini beans		Millet	Flaxseeds
Edamame (young soybeans)		Whole wheat grain	Hemp seeds (complete protein)
			Pumpkin seeds
			Sunflower seeds
			Nut butters (e.g., peanut, almond)

Where I and many others go wrong (it's something I have struggled with) is constant snacking and grazing between meals. If you can eat good-quality high-protein meals throughout the day, the cravings and dependency on sugar passes and the food noise quietens. When this happens you are winning and may start to see your body changing.

As I've mentioned, protein helps us all feel fuller for longer and helps stabilise our blood glucose levels. If we consume a healthy, protein-fuelled breakfast, lunch and dinner, then we will stop relying on snacks to keep us going. Shifting to this mindset and considering batch cooking, meal prepping and taking your own food to work will change your life. It's not always easy – there are times I get caught out and have a whole day of eating UPFs – but those days are rarer than ever for me because I constantly remind myself of how much better I feel when I eat real, healthy, home-cooked food, or a healthy snack: maybe a piece of fruit, a handful of unsalted nuts and seeds, or some plain Greek yoghurt – all these can help give you an energy boost.

Another idea I like to share is this: breakfast doesn't have to look like breakfast. When most people think about breakfast foods, it's usually things like cereal, muesli, granola, fruit, yoghurt, juice, toast with jam, pancakes, waffles or pastries. While there is generally nothing wrong with these, they don't lead with protein and tend to be high in sugar, which spikes your blood glucose levels and leaves you feeling hungry an hour later. Why not shift this mindset and have some leftover dinner from the night before instead (ideally with some veg), something savoury and delicious that doesn't 'look' like breakfast but which actually fuels your body in a healthy way and has all the wonderful benefits of a high-protein meal.

A little bit on nutrition

You'll notice that I haven't included the calorie content for the recipes in this book. I've always believed that the most important thing to focus on should be the cooking. For many people, just finding the time to consistently cook from scratch at home is a big enough challenge by itself, so I don't want to throw in another thing to think about by suggesting you track, weigh and count every calorie each day.

I have never calculated my calorie intake, but I know that if I reduce snacking and cut out sweet treats, fizzy drinks and daily puddings, I naturally start to create a calorie deficit and lose body fat.

I haven't included a full macronutrient breakdown in the recipes, but I have highlighted the protein content in grams per recipe. I'm hoping this will help educate you on which type of meals contain the most, and also help you with meal planning for the week ahead.

Just like I don't promote or encourage calorie counting or getting people to focus on a daily calorie target, I also don't believe it's essential to have a daily protein target. As long as you are aware of which recipes are higher in protein and which are lower, it will all work itself out. Every day your protein intake will be different, but as long as you have variety in your week, you'll be getting plenty of protein in your diet. And remember, your protein needs vary throughout your life.

I've packed as much protein as I can into the 80 recipes, of which 17 are vegetarian and 4 are vegan. It is more challenging to produce high-protein recipes without animal protein, so you may notice some of the vegetarian and vegan recipes have lower protein counts than the others. Again, this is fine. Some days I eat a much higher-protein diet than others. No two days are ever the same. Focus on variety and you'll be just fine. It's important to eat intuitively where you can and learn to listen to your body more. It's unlikely you will ever over-consume protein – give these recipes a try and you'll get into a good rhythm and get a sense of how much you need to eat.

All of the recipes are classified as 'higher protein' and most are 'high protein' (the UK government currently defines 'higher protein' as deriving 20 per cent of the energy of a meal from protein).

I have also included helpful 'protein boosts' throughout, in case you want to hack the protein count. For instance, I'm not a massive quinoa fan – I'd probably use rice instead – but if you like quinoa and want to pump up the protein, you can make a swap. These cheeky little protein tips will really boost your intake over the week, so they can be super handy.

What I want you to take away from this book

I hope this book inspires you to fall in love with cooking again. I want it to motivate you to change your diet in a positive way, from adapting your food shopping, to improving your meal planning and your overall health. We are what we eat, and I think now more than ever we need to be taking care of ourselves. This can't be achieved with exercise and sleep alone. The most powerful, energising and healing thing we can use to feel different is food and nutrition.

I hope you love the recipes and you get the kids or grandkids involved with learning to cook, too. It's such an important life skill, but also a wonderful way to bond and connect with each other.

Next time you are having bad day and are really craving a treat, try to start off by having a balanced meal containing protein first. It will help mitigate that craving. But if you still want to eat UPFs once in a while, that's okay – what you eat day-in day-out makes far more of a difference to your health than an occasional UPF. Remind yourself that healthy food is the treat. That's the reward you really deserve, because UPFs only bring us down – after the dopamine high comes the dopamine low, and that has a massive impact on our mood.

I know the prospect of eating more whole foods and fewer UPFs can be daunting, and often worrying because of the cost associated with healthy food. There is no denying that poor-quality food is cheap and it can feel unachievable and almost impossible to cut it out completely, so rather than being hard on yourself or feeling guilty just focus on reducing it one day at a time.

Finally, I'd love to invite you to try my 7-day WHOLE FOOD CHALLENGE: spend a week eating real food from this book. You will feel absolutely incredible if you do. Simply plan your breakfast, lunches and dinners into the week and get cooking. Fancy the challenge?

'GOOD FOOD, GOOD MOOD'

'PROTEIN *is* IMPORTANT FOR US ALL, REGARDLESS *of* AGE, GENDER *or* LIFESTYLE'

'EAT *to* FEEL AWESOME'

JOE'S HOME 'TAKEAWAYS'

Silly Dilly Salmon Burger

SERVES

4

PREP: 15 mins
COOK: 15 mins

4 skinless salmon fillets (see Tip on page 159), about 150g each, cut into rough chunks
4 tbsp shop-bought dried breadcrumbs
generous handful of dill fronds, chopped
finely grated zest of 1 lemon (preferably unwaxed)
½ tbsp olive oil, plus extra for drizzling
50g curly kale, roughly chopped
salt and freshly ground black pepper

For the dill and caper cream

150g crème fraîche
handful of dill fronds, chopped
2 tbsp baby capers, drained, plus 1–2 tsp of the brine

To assemble

4 seeded buns, halved and buttered
4 thick slices of large (beef) tomato

This is phenomenal. Fish burgers can sometimes be dry and barren but not this one. It's the opposite. The dill and caper cream tastes unreal and keeps the whole burger so juicy. This could possibly be the best-tasting burger in this book, but I'll let you decide that for yourself.

Preheat the oven to 200°C (180°C fan/gas mark 6) and line two medium baking trays with baking paper.

Finely chop the salmon chunks until they are completely minced. Tip into a bowl and add the breadcrumbs, dill and lemon zest. Season with salt and pepper, then shape into four large, compact patties.

Place the patties onto one of the lined baking trays and bake in the oven for 8–9 minutes until cooked through, then remove from the oven and drizzle with a little olive oil. Do not turn off the oven.

For the crispy kale, drizzle the ½ tablespoon of olive oil over the kale in a bowl and season lightly with salt. Mix well to coat, using your hands to massage the oil evenly into the kale. Spread the kale out on the second baking tray and crisp it up in the hot oven for no longer than 3 minutes.

To make the dill and caper cream, combine the crème fraîche, dill and capers in a bowl. Season with pepper and adjust the salty seasoning (and consistency) by adding a teaspoon or two of the caper brine juice. Set aside.

Spread the dill and caper cream evenly over both the top and bottom halves of all 4 of your buns. Place the crispy kale on the bottom half, top with a juicy slice of tomato and then a salmon patty before adding the top half of the bun. Serve immediately, with any leftover dill and caper cream on the side.

Fantastic Frickin' Chickin Burger

SERVES

4

swap the soy sauce for tamari & use GF buns

I'm really spicing things up with this one. Expect a proper flavour explosion when you get your laughing gear round this and take the first bite. It hits different. No bland chicken and dry buns here. I've gone for a delicious ginger, sesame and cucumber topping. It's worth the extra love and beats a dollop of ketchup hands down.

PREP: 15 mins
COOK: 25 mins, *plus resting*

4 large skinless, boneless
   chicken thighs
1 tsp chilli powder
1 tsp garlic powder
drizzle of olive oil
salt and freshly ground
   black pepper

For the ginger and cucumber topping

½ large cucumber
1 tbsp rice wine vinegar
1½ tsp toasted sesame oil
1 tsp white sesame seeds
10g fresh ginger, finely grated
1 garlic clove, crushed

To serve

60g mayonnaise
1 tsp soy sauce
4 seeded buns, buttered
4 leaves of little gem lettuce
4 leaves of butter lettuce
1 ripe avocado, stoned, peeled
   and thinly sliced
small squeeze of lemon juice
handful of coriander leaves
¼ small red onion, thinly sliced

Preheat the oven to 220°C (200°C fan/gas mark 7) and line a baking tray with baking paper.

Put the chicken thighs in a large bowl, scatter over the chilli and garlic powders and season with salt and pepper. Drizzle over the olive oil, then get stuck in with clean hands, massaging the seasoning evenly into the chicken. Spread out the chicken thighs on the lined baking tray and bake in the oven for 20–22 minutes, until cooked through. Set aside to rest, covered with foil, for at least 8–10 minutes.

Meanwhile, pull a vegetable peeler along the length of the half cucumber, held over a bowl, to shave it into long ribbons, turning it as you go – stop when you get to the very seedy, watery core. Add the remaining ingredients for the ginger and cucumber topping to the bowl, along with a small pinch of salt, and mix well to combine. Just before serving, tip into a sieve to drain off any excess moisture.

To assemble the burgers, make a quick dressing by mixing the mayo and soy sauce in a small bowl. Spread this mixture evenly over both the top and bottom halves of all the buns. Add both types of lettuce and the chicken and place generous mounds of the drained cucumber and ginger topping on top of the chicken. Place the avocado slices on top of the cucumber, squeeze over the lemon juice and season the avo with salt and pepper. Top with the coriander and red onion slices, then top with the other half of the bun. Serve any leftover mayo dressing on the side.

Tip

Swap the chicken with the salmon patties on page 25 for a twist. (If you do, add a little chilli powder to the salmon patty mix for a spicy kick.)

Wide Open Steak Sarnie

SERVES

4

PREP: 15 mins
COOK: 10 mins, *plus resting*

4 sirloin steaks, visible fat
    removed
130g baby plum tomatoes,
    chopped
1 large garlic clove, crushed
3 thyme sprigs, leaves picked
2 tbsp olive oil, plus extra for
    drizzling
generous pinch of dried
    oregano
40g wild rocket
4 slices of toasted sourdough,
    buttered
120g creamy blue cheese, cut
    into pieces (4–5 small pieces
    per sandwich)
salt and freshly ground
    black pepper

This is a thing of beauty. Look at it. Imagine that in your hands right now. You may not love the blue cheese vibes like I do. All good. You could swap it for any cheese you like: cream cheese, feta, mozzarella, Parmesan or a classic cheddar will all do the job. Do make the garlicky tomatoes though, because they really cap it off so well.

Remove the steaks from the fridge 30 minutes before cooking.

Combine the chopped tomatoes, garlic and thyme leaves in a small bowl. Season with salt and pepper and stir in 1 tablespoon of the olive oil. Mix well and set aside.

Season the steaks with salt and pepper, then heat the other tablespoon of oil in a large frying pan over a high heat. Add the steaks and cook for 2 minutes on each side (for medium). Cook for 45–60 seconds longer on each side for thicker cuts, or longer still if you prefer your steaks more well-done. Cook two steaks at a time if needed, to avoid overcrowding the pan. Set the steaks aside on a clean chopping board, sprinkle with the oregano and cover with foil. Leave to rest for 8–10 minutes before slicing.

Drizzle 1–2 teaspoons of oil over the rocket in a bowl, season with salt and toss to lightly coat.

Divide the dressed rocket among the buttered, toasted sourdough and top with the sliced steak. Evenly scatter pieces of creamy blue cheese over the steaks, then spoon on the tomato mix. Season with more salt and pepper, if needed. Serve immediately.

Thai Me Up, Baby

SERVES

4

PREP: 10 mins
COOK: 25 mins

100g creamed coconut block, roughly chopped

10g desiccated coconut

4 large skinless, boneless chicken breasts, or 8 large skinless, boneless chicken thighs (about 800g), roughly chopped

1 tsp ground ginger

1 tsp garlic powder

2–3 tbsp olive oil, plus extra for drizzling

1 aubergine, cut into 1–2cm dice

170g green Thai curry paste

1 x 400g tin chickpeas, drained and rinsed

280g uncooked basmati rice

salt and freshly ground black pepper

To serve

1 red chilli, thinly sliced (deseeded if preferred)

handful of coriander leaves, chopped

1 lime, cut into wedges or cheeks

If you ever find yourself craving a takeaway, give this recipe a go. It's simple and delicious. Avoid the tinned coconut milks, which often contain gums and emulsifiers, and instead opt for the solid block of creamed coconut, which is 99.9% pure coconut. The great thing with curries like this is you can really throw in any of your favourite veg. So, if you don't enjoy the texture of aubergine, you could use courgette, baby corn or mangetout. Whatever you go for, it's guaranteed to taste incredible.

Add 400ml boiling-hot water to a heatproof jug and add the creamed coconut pieces. Leave to dissolve, whisking if necessary.

Toast the desiccated coconut in a dry frying pan over a medium-high heat for 3–4 minutes until golden, stirring regularly (be careful: it can burn quickly). Set aside in a bowl.

Add the chopped chicken to a large bowl and sprinkle over the ginger and garlic. Toss well to evenly coat.

Heat a tablespoon of oil in a large frying pan or wok over a high heat. Fry the chicken in batches for 4–5 minutes per batch until golden brown all over, adding another tablespoon of oil for each batch. Transfer to a bowl, season and set aside.

Add more oil to the same pan over a medium-high heat, add the aubergine and stir-fry for 3–4 minutes until softened and starting to caramelise. Reduce the heat to medium and add the curry paste and coconut milk. Bring to the boil and let it cook for several minutes until the coconut milk reduces by more than half.

Reduce the heat to low, add the rinsed chickpeas and return the chicken pieces to the pan (along with any juices from the bowl). Leave to warm through until ready to serve.

Meanwhile, cook the rice according to the packet instructions (usually in a saucepan of boiling water for 10–15 minutes). Once cooked, drain the rice in a sieve and season with salt. Stir through half the toasted coconut.

Serve the chicken with the rice, scattering over the remaining coconut. Top the chicken with sliced chilli and coriander and serve with lime wedges or cheeks on the side to squeeze over.

Thai Prawn Curry with Spiced Quinoa

SERVES

4

swap the
soy sauce
for tamari

PREP: 15 mins
COOK: 20 mins

100g creamed coconut block,
  roughly chopped (see Tip)
1 tbsp coconut oil or olive oil
1 onion, finely chopped
4 garlic cloves, crushed
50g red Thai curry paste
600g raw, shelled king prawns,
  defrosted if frozen
1 tbsp soy sauce
1 tsp fish sauce
juice of 1 lime (about 2 tsp)
100g mangetout
100g shelled edamame beans
  (defrosted if frozen)
1 tsp honey
100g cherry tomatoes, halved
generous handful of coriander
  leaves, chopped
1 lime, cut into wedges, to serve

For the spicy sesame quinoa

400ml fish stock (ideally fresh)
200g quinoa, rinsed
3 tbsp white sesame seeds
1 tsp dried chilli flakes
salt and freshly ground
  black pepper

This fantastic curry is full of beautiful flavours. If you haven't prepared quinoa before, I really think you should try it, and adding the fish stock, sesame seeds and chilli flakes takes it to a new level of flavour.

Add 400ml boiling-hot water to a heatproof jug and add the creamed coconut pieces. Leave to dissolve, whisking if necessary.

Heat the oil of your choice in a large frying pan or wok over a medium heat. Add the onion and cook for 3–4 minutes until soft and translucent, then stir in the garlic and cook for another minute. Remove half the cooked onion mixture and set aside in a small bowl (you will add it to the quinoa later).

To the same pan (containing the remaining onion), add the curry paste and cook for 1 minute, then pour in the prepared coconut milk. Simmer over a high heat for 3–4 minutes until the coconut milk reduces and thickens. This is important, as the creamy sauce will thin out again once the prawns and vegetables are added.

Once thickened, reduce the heat to medium and add the prawns, soy sauce, fish sauce and lime juice. Stir well, then add the mangetout and edamame. Simmer for 5–6 minutes until the prawns are pink and opaque, stirring so they cook evenly. Stir through the honey and tomatoes, then remove from the heat.

At the same time, cook the quinoa. Bring the stock to the boil in a large saucepan. Add the quinoa, reduce the heat to medium, cover partially with a lid and simmer for 12–15 minutes until the water is absorbed and the pan is dry. Check it regularly – the quinoa is cooked when the grains are translucent and the outer germ separates. Fluff with a fork and stir in the onion mixture you set aside earlier, with the sesame seeds and chilli flakes. Season to taste with salt and pepper.

To serve, divide the quinoa among four warm bowls and ladle over the curry. Garnish with the coriander and serve with the lime wedges.

Tip

Creamed coconut makes this beautifully rich, but swap in a 400g tin of full-fat coconut milk if you prefer.

Don't like quinoa? Use rice, flavouring it the same way.

Nacho Average Prawn Tacos

SERVES

4

makes 12 tacos

PREP: 15 mins
COOK: 15 mins

2 tbsp olive oil
½ onion, finely chopped
2 garlic cloves, crushed
1 red chilli, finely chopped
   (deseeded if preferred)
200g baby plum tomatoes,
   finely chopped
1 tsp dried oregano
½ tsp ground cumin
¼ tsp ground cinnamon
450g raw, shelled king prawns,
   defrosted if frozen
2 limes (preferably unwaxed)
12 hard taco shells
small handful of coriander
   leaves, chopped
salt and freshly ground
   black pepper

**For the soured cream and
avocado guacamole**

2 ripe avocados, stoned, peeled
   and roughly chopped
juice of 2 limes (about 1 tbsp)
60g soured cream
generous pinch of dried chilli
   flakes, plus extra to serve
small handful of coriander
   leaves, chopped
2 little gem lettuces, trimmed
   and thinly sliced

**These are not average. They're holy moly guacamole good.
I love making them with my kids. There's something so fun and
satisfying about building your very own dream taco when it's
all laid out on the table, self-serve style. Enjoy!**

Heat the oil in a large frying pan or wok over a medium heat.
Add the onion, garlic and chilli and cook gently for 2–3 minutes,
then stir in the chopped tomatoes, dried oregano, cumin and
cinnamon and cook for a further 2–3 minutes. Increase the heat
to medium-high, add the prawns and cook, stirring continuously,
for 3–4 minutes until the prawns are pink and opaque. Transfer
the whole lot to a large bowl and finely grate in the zest of both
limes. Season with salt and pepper and stir well to combine.
Place the mixture into a large sieve set over a bowl to drain
away excess moisture. Cut the zested limes into cheeks or slices,
for serving.

To make the soured cream and avocado mix, mash the
avocados with the lime juice in a bowl, using a fork. Stir in the
soured cream, chilli flakes and chopped coriander and season
with salt and pepper. Tip in the sliced lettuce and mix to evenly
combine. The mixture will be thick and chunky, but that's what
you are going for!

Fill the tacos equally with the avocado and lettuce mix (around
40g in each), followed by the prawn mix (3–4 prawns/40–45g in
each). Finish with more chopped coriander and a small pinch of
chilli flakes. Serve with the zested lime wedges to squeeze over.

Korean-style chicken tacos (per taco)

If you have any taco shells kicking about, add a little shredded lettuce, 30g Slow-cooked Shredded Chicken (see page 184) and 20g drained kimchi. Sprinkle over some chopped coriander and you are good to go!

Beefy Tex-Mex-style tacos (per taco)

As above, fill a taco shell with some shredded lettuce. Add 40g of the Mexican-style Beef Stew with Rice (see page 203) and top with grated cheese, a spoonful of soured cream and some sliced chillies. If you have coriander kicking about, add it as a fresh garnish.

What Did the Chicken Satay? Eat Me!

SERVES

4

swap the
soy sauce
for tamari

PREP: 15 mins
COOK: 25 mins, plus resting

4 large skinless, boneless
chicken breasts, cut into long,
thin strips
1 tbsp curry powder
2 tsp red Thai curry paste
1 tsp honey
olive oil, for drizzling
3 tbsp white sesame seeds
4 x 125g packets of ready-
cooked basmati rice
salt and ground black pepper

For the peanut sauce

70g creamed coconut block,
roughly chopped
1½ tbsp red Thai curry paste
150g smooth peanut butter
1 tbsp plus 2 tsp honey
1½ tsp soy sauce
½ tsp apple cider vinegar

For the cucumber salad

3–4 baby cucumbers, sliced
1 red chilli, thinly sliced
2 tsp rice wine vinegar
1 tsp white sesame seeds

To serve

30g roasted peanuts, chopped
handful of coriander leaves
1 lime, cut into wedges or cheeks

I'm a sucker for anything peanutty. I've perfected this satay sauce over the past few years – it's very good, and will really blow your socks off, not because it's spicy but because it tastes so yummy. Adding sesame seeds to your plain old rice is also a great trick to add extra flavour.

Preheat the oven to 220°C (200°C fan/gas mark 7) and line a large baking tray with baking paper.

Put the chicken strips in a large bowl, sprinkle over the curry powder and add the curry paste, honey and a drizzle of olive oil. Season with salt and pepper, then massage the seasoning into the chicken with clean hands. Thread the strips of chicken onto skewers, gently weaving the skewer in and out of each strip of meat, so the chicken folds back and forth along the skewer, don't compact it too tightly – a little space helps it cook through evenly. Place the skewers on the baking tray and bake in the oven for 20–23 minutes, until cooked through (see skewer tip on p52).

Add 280ml boiling-hot water to a heatproof jug and add the creamed coconut pieces. Whisk to dissolve. Add the coconut milk to a large saucepan with the curry paste, peanut butter, honey, soy sauce and apple cider vinegar. Simmer over a medium heat for 2-3 minutes, whisking well. The sauce should be thick but still pourable. If it's too thick, whisk in a dash of water; if it's too thin, leave it over the heat a little longer to reduce and thicken.

Meanwhile, prepare the rice. Toast the sesame seeds in a large, dry frying pan over a medium-high heat for 3–4 minutes until golden, stirring occasionally. Add the cooked rice and a splash of water and gently reheat. Season and keep warm.

For the cucumber salad, combine all the ingredients in a bowl.

Serve the chicken with the rice, peanut sauce and salad. Scatter with the peanuts and coriander and serve with lime wedges or cheeks to squeeze over.

Ginger Chicken with Egg-fried Rice

SERVES

4

swap the soy sauce for tamari

PREP: 15 mins
COOK: 20 mins

2 tbsp coconut oil or olive oil
4 large skinless, boneless chicken breasts, or 8 large skinless, boneless chicken thighs (about 800g), sliced
30g fresh ginger, finely grated
2 garlic cloves, crushed
200g chestnut mushrooms, thickly sliced
200g savoy cabbage, shredded or thinly sliced
3 tbsp oyster sauce

For the egg-fried rice

200g uncooked basmati rice
drizzle of olive oil
1 garlic clove, crushed
6 spring onions, trimmed and thinly sliced
4 eggs, whisked
2 tbsp soy sauce
¼ tsp dried chilli flakes
2 tbsp toasted sesame oil

To serve

1 tbsp toasted sesame seeds
1 red chilli, thinly sliced (deseeded if preferred)

I've always been a big fan of stir-fries – they're so speedy and simple. And when you get it right, you can absolutely pack them with flavour, too. Ginger and oyster sauce are the heroes here, and combined with savoy cabbage, it's just the best, and the egg-fried rice adds some extra protein. I could eat this a couple of nights a week, no problem. Give it a go!

Heat 1 tablespoon of oil in a large frying pan or wok over a high heat, add half the chicken strips and cook for 4–5 minutes until golden brown all over. Remove from the pan and set aside in a bowl, then add the other tablespoon of oil and brown the remaining strips, transferring them to the same bowl. Season with salt and pepper and set aside.

Add the ginger, garlic, mushrooms and cabbage to the still-hot pan (adding more oil, if needed) and stir-fry for 5–6 minutes until tender, stirring to avoid burning the garlic.

Return the chicken pieces to the pan (along with any juices from the bowl) and stir through the oyster sauce. Simmer for about 5 minutes over a low heat until the sauce coats the mixture and the chicken is cooked through. Keep warm.

Meanwhile, make the egg-fried rice. Cook the rice according to the packet instructions (usually in a saucepan of boiling water for 10–15 minutes). Once cooked, drain the rice in a sieve.

Heat a drizzle of olive oil in a large frying pan or wok over a medium heat, add the garlic and spring onions and cook for 1–2 minutes, then add the whisked eggs and cook for 20–30 seconds – stirring regularly – until scrambled. Tip in the drained rice and stir in the soy sauce and chilli flakes. Stir vigorously to combine, then remove from the heat. Add the sesame oil and stir again to combine.

Divide the egg-fried rice among four warm plates or bowls and add equal amounts of the flavour-packed saucy chicken mixture. Scatter over the sesame seeds and sliced chilli and enjoy!

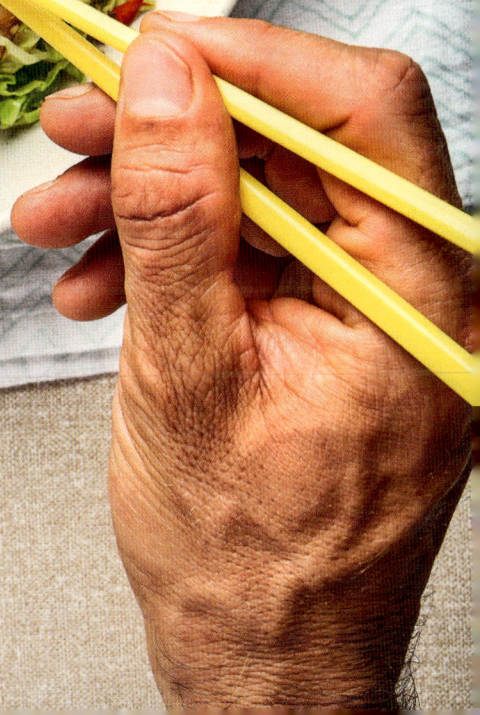

Buffalo Joe's Chicken Bowl

SERVES

4

raw burger
patties only

PREP: 15 mins
COOK: 30 mins, _plus resting_

4 large skinless, boneless
   chicken breasts
1 tsp garlic powder
1 tsp smoked paprika
drizzle of olive oil
60g hot peri-peri sauce (like
   Nando's®)
50g walnuts
4 little gem lettuces, trimmed
   and thinly sliced
2 celery stalks, finely chopped
70g blue cheese, crumbled
¼ red onion, very thinly sliced
salt and freshly ground
   black pepper

For the 'ranch' dressing

100g plain (natural) yoghurt,
   preferably Greek yoghurt
½ tsp Dijon mustard
1 garlic clove, crushed

Saddle up cowboy and let's hit the ranch. This version is delicious and much healthier than any shop-bought ultra-processed ranch dressing. The blue cheese may not be your vibe, but I just love it. Feel free to swap it for any cheese of your choice. This is a great one to have as a lunch on the go, too.

Preheat the oven to 220°C (200°C fan/gas mark 7) and line both a large baking tray and a smaller tray with baking paper.

Place the chicken breasts on the large lined baking tray and season with a little salt and a very generous crack of black pepper. Scatter over the garlic powder and smoked paprika. Drizzle with the olive oil and brush the seasoning on evenly. Bake in the oven for 15 minutes, then remove from the oven and brush over all the peri-peri sauce. Bake for another 5–6 minutes, until cooked through. Set aside to rest, covered with foil, for at least 8–10 minutes. Just before serving, cut into 1–1.5cm-thick slices.

While the chicken is resting, reduce the oven temperature to 190°C (170°C fan/gas mark 5) and spread the walnuts out on the smaller lined tray. Toast them in the oven for 8–10 minutes, then set aside to cool before roughly chopping.

Make the dressing by whisking together all the ingredients in a small bowl. Season with salt and pepper.

Combine the lettuce and celery in a large bowl, add a drizzle of olive oil and season with salt. Divide the seasoned lettuce among four plates or bowls. Top with the sliced chicken and spoon over the 'ranch' dressing, finishing with the blue cheese, red onion and toasted walnuts: so good!

Enjoy immediately. You can also store the salad and cooked chicken in the fridge in an airtight container for up to 3–4 days, keeping the dressing, cheese and nuts separately and adding just before serving.

Tip

Air-fry the walnuts at 190°C for 5–6 minutes until golden, shaking the basket halfway through.

The whole mix makes great wraps using soft tortillas!

Joe's Cowboy Burger

SERVES

4

PREP: 15 mins
COOK: 15 mins

For the patties

600g minced beef
1 tsp ground cumin
1 tsp garlic powder
½ tsp dried oregano
1 tbsp double-concentrated
    tomato puree
2 tbsp olive oil
salt and freshly ground
    black pepper

For Joe's 'cowboy' relish

50g frozen sweetcorn kernels
6 spring onions, trimmed and
    thinly sliced
3 garlic cloves, crushed
2 tbsp Dijon mustard
2 tsp Worcestershire sauce
2 tsp dried chilli flakes
1 tsp smoked paprika
generous handful of coriander
    leaves, finely chopped
40g mayonnaise
juice and finely grated zest of
    1 lemon (preferably unwaxed)

To serve

4–8 butter lettuce leaves
4 seeded buns, halved and
    buttered
4 thick slices of large (beef)
    tomato

I've always said that my favourite food on earth is a burger. I just don't think anything comes close to the joy and satisfaction of slapping a patty between two buns and noshing it off, and this one is up there for me. The spiced beef patties have proper flavour and the cowboy corn relish might look like a faff, but trust me, it's worth it and really turns this burger into something special. Move over tomato ketchup, there's a new sheriff in town.

Put the minced beef in a large bowl and sprinkle over the cumin, garlic powder and oregano. Add the tomato puree and season generously with salt and pepper. Get stuck in with clean hands, mixing to combine, then divide into four equal-sized portions and shape into large, flat patties. These can be set aside for now in the fridge (or frozen, if you want to make them ahead of time).

Meanwhile make the relish. Cook the corn in a small saucepan of boiling water for 3–4 minutes until tender. Drain and leave to cool, then add to a bowl with the remaining ingredients, mixing well to combine. Season with salt and pepper.

To cook the patties, heat the oil in a large frying pan over a high heat. Add the patties and fry for about 3 minutes on each side, until golden and caramelised. Turn the heat down to low, cover the pan with a lid and leave to cook through for another 3–4 minutes. Set aside.

To serve, lay the soft lettuce leaves on the base of each burger bun. Top with a dollop of the cowboy relish, add a slice of tomato and a cooked patty. Spread over more cowboy relish, then cover with the top half of the bun.

Tip

To air-fry the patties, brush each patty with olive oil and cook in the air fryer at 190°C for 7–8 minutes until cooked through.

PROTEIN BOOST

Top each patty with a fried egg!

Bangin' Beef Stir-fry

SERVES

4

PREP: 10 mins, *plus*
10 mins marinating
COOK: 15 mins

4 sirloin steaks, visible fat
    removed (or 700g shop-
    bought beef stir-fry strips)
3 tbsp low-sodium soy sauce
2 tsp ground ginger
freshly ground black pepper

For the sauce

2 tbsp hoisin sauce
2 tbsp rice wine vinegar
1 tsp toasted sesame oil
1 tsp dried chilli flakes
½ tsp smoked paprika

For the stir-fry

2–3 tbsp coconut oil or olive oil
250g shiitake mushrooms, sliced
1 red pepper, deseeded and
    sliced
2 pak choy (or 4 baby pak choi),
    trimmed and roughly sliced
2 spring onions, trimmed and
    thinly sliced
2 garlic cloves, crushed
2 tbsp toasted sesame oil
4 nests dried egg noodles

To serve

1 red chilli, thinly sliced
2 tsp white sesame seeds
handful of coriander leaves
1 lime, cut into wedges

As far as stir-fries go, this is well up there as one of my faves. Who needs to order a greasy takeaway when you can make stuff like this at home. The sauce tastes bangin' with the steak, but it also works well with chicken. If you want to mix this up a bit, you could always serve it with some jasmine rice instead of noodles.

Remove the meat from the fridge 30 minutes before cooking, and cut it into 1cm-thick strips (if not using pre-sliced steak).

Mix the beef with the soy sauce and ground ginger in a bowl, season with black pepper and toss to coat. Set aside to marinate for about 10 minutes.

Meanwhile, make the sauce by whisking together all the ingredients in a small bowl.

For the stir-fry, heat 1 tablespoon of the oil in a large frying pan or wok over a high heat, then add half the beef and fry for about 2 minutes until browned all over. Remove from the pan, set aside, and fry the remaining beef, adding more oil if needed. Transfer the second batch of beef to the bowl.

Add a little more oil to the same pan and place over a medium-high heat. Tip in the mushrooms, pepper, pak choy and half the spring onions and stir-fry for 4–5 minutes, adding the garlic in the last 1 minute, until everything is slightly tender. Reduce the heat to low and return all the beef to the pan (along with any juices from the bowl). Pour in the sauce, toss everything together and cook gently for 1–2 minutes until the sauce thickens and coats the beef and vegetables. Remove from the heat and drizzle over 1 tablespoon of the sesame oil, mixing it in well.

Cook the noodles according to the packet instructions. Drain well and toss with the remaining 1 tablespoon of sesame oil.

Divide the noodles among warm bowls. Ladle over the beef and veg mix, then scatter with the sliced chilli, remaining spring onion, sesame seeds and coriander. Serve with the lime wedges.

El Burrito Fantastico

SERVES

4

PREP: 15 mins
COOK: 20 mins

3 sirloin steaks, visible fat
removed (or the equivalent
weight of shop-bought beef
stir-fry strips)
2–3 tbsp olive oil
1 onion, finely chopped
1 red pepper, deseeded and
thinly sliced
2 garlic cloves, crushed
2 tsp dried oregano
200ml beef stock (made with
½ stock cube)
200ml passata
1 tbsp double-concentrated
tomato puree
1 bay leaf
1 x 400g tin black beans,
drained and rinsed
juice of 1 lime (about 2 tsp)
30g pickled jalapeño slices
(drained weight), finely
chopped
salt and freshly ground
black pepper

To assemble

4 soft high-protein tortillas
50g extra-mature cheddar
cheese, finely grated
4 tbsp soured cream
handful of coriander leaves,
chopped

I think I've perfected the ultimate Mexican-style burrito.
No dry beef strips here – the steak simmers in a rich tomatoey
sauce with black beans and a good kick of jalapeño. It's the
sort of thing you inhale, then immediately want to rack up
another one. I highly recommend this one any day of
the week.

Remove the meat from the fridge 30 minutes before cooking,
and cut it into 1cm-thick strips (if not using pre-sliced steak).

Heat 1 tablespoon of the oil in a large frying pan or wok over a
high heat, then add half the beef strips and cook for 2–3 minutes
until brown on all sides. Remove from the pan, set aside in a
bowl, and cook the remaining beef, adding more oil. Transfer the
second batch of beef to the bowl. Season with salt and pepper
and set aside.

Add a little more oil to the same pan and place over a medium
heat. Add the onion and red pepper and cook for 3–4 minutes
until slightly softened, then stir in the garlic and oregano and
cook for another minute. Add the stock, passata, tomato puree
and bay leaf and simmer for 4–5 minutes until the mixture
thickens. Add the beans, then return the beef to the pan (along
with any juices from the bowl) and warm through for 2–3
minutes. The mixture should be thick and chunky. Remove from
the heat and discard the bay leaf. Season with salt and stir in
the lime juice and jalapeño.

Divide the beef mix evenly among 4 tortillas. Top with equal
amounts of cheese, soured cream and coriander. Fold in the
sides of the tortilla, then roll tightly from the bottom up. If you're
making them ahead, wrap in foil and keep in the fridge.

Tip

Any beefy mix left over after making your tortillas is great the next day on a baked potato!

Tip

If using wooden skewers, soak them in water ahead of time: this prevents them burning in the oven.

Lovely Lamb Koftas

SERVES

4

PREP: 15 mins
COOK: 20 mins

For the koftas

500g minced lamb
1 tsp onion powder (or granules)
1 tsp garlic powder
1 tsp ground cumin
1 tsp ground coriander
½ tsp ground paprika
½ tsp ground cinnamon
½ tsp dried oregano
½ tsp dried chilli flakes
handful of mint leaves,
    finely chopped
1 tbsp olive oil
salt and freshly ground
    black pepper

For the tzatziki

½ cucumber, grated and
    drained well in a sieve
180g plain (natural) yoghurt,
    preferably Greek yoghurt
1 garlic clove, crushed
juice of ½ lemon (about 1 tbsp)
generous handful of mint
    leaves, finely chopped

To assemble

4 soft high-protein tortillas
60g baby plum tomatoes, thinly
    sliced

I don't often cook lamb, but when I do, I always go for these and my kids are totally chuffed: they love eating the koftas and getting involved helping me make the tzatziki. It's such a lovely, simple, fresh thing to make. Lamb and tzatziki make the perfect pair and when you throw it in a wrap, it's a right delicious mouthful.

Preheat the oven to 220°C (200°C fan/gas mark 7) and line a large baking tray with baking paper.

Combine all the ingredients for the koftas (apart from the olive oil) in a large bowl, season with salt and pepper and mix well to evenly combine. Divide the seasoned mince into four portions (125–130g each) and shape the mixture around a skewer in a long, cylinder shape 10–12cm long – make sure they are an even thickness. Place the skewer on the lined baking tray and repeat until all four are made, then drizzle over a little olive oil and brush the oil over evenly. Bake in the oven for 17–18 minutes until cooked through. Set aside.

Meanwhile, make the tzatziki. Press the cucumber in the sieve to help remove all the excess water. Combine the yoghurt, drained cucumber, garlic, lemon juice and most of the mint. Season with salt and pepper, mixing well to combine.

To assemble the wraps, divide the tzatziki evenly among four tortillas. Slide the cooked lamb off the skewers and place on top of the tzatziki. Add the sliced tomatoes and finish with a scattering of the remaining chopped mint. Add another crack of pepper for good measure, then fold in the sides of the tortilla, rolling tightly from the bottom up.

EASY PEASY DINNERS

Cheesy Baked Eggs with Ham

SERVES

4

PREP: 10 mins
COOK: 20 mins

1 tbsp olive oil, plus extra for
greasing
300g baby spinach
3 garlic cloves, crushed
80g crème fraîche
pinch of ground nutmeg
(optional)
300g deli ham, roughly
chopped
4 eggs
50g gruyère cheese, finely
grated
handful of chives, snipped or
finely chopped (optional)
salt and freshly ground
black pepper
4 slices of toasted sourdough,
to serve

Eggs on toast or ham and cheese omelettes are a classic daily breakfast in our house. Sometimes it's nice to make a bit more effort with your eggs, and this is a really tasty and easy, protein-rich option. There's very little prep, which leaves time to fit in a quick 20-minute workout while it's in the oven.

Preheat the oven to 200°C (180°C fan/gas mark 6) and grease a deep, medium ovenproof baking dish (like a lasagne dish) with a little oil.

Heat the 1 tablespoon of oil in a large frying pan or wok over a medium-high heat, then add the spinach and cook for 2–3 minutes until the spinach has completely wilted and the pan is dry. Add the garlic and cook for another 1–2 minutes, stirring continuously to prevent the garlic burning. Tip in the crème fraîche and season with salt and pepper (and a small pinch of nutmeg, if using). Remove the pan from the heat and mix in the chopped ham.

Transfer the creamy spinach and ham mix to the greased baking dish. Make four small wells in the mixture and crack an egg into each well.

Scatter over the grated gruyère, then bake in the oven for 15–16 minutes, or until the egg whites are set. If you like firm yolks, bake for an extra 2–3 minutes.

Remove from the oven, top with fresh chives (if using) and take to the table as is. Allow everyone to tuck in and have some slices of toasted sourdough at hand to enjoy alongside.

Buttered-up Salmon and Veg

SERVES

4

PREP: 10 mins
COOK: 20 mins

750g baby potatoes, halved (larger ones quartered, to ensure even cooking)
200g asparagus spears, trimmed
200g Tenderstem® broccoli (long-stem/broccolini)
4 salmon fillets (about 600g in total)
drizzle of olive oil
salt and freshly ground black pepper
1 lemon, cut into wedges or cheeks, to serve

For the garlic and parsley butter

20g unsalted butter
1 garlic clove, crushed
handful of parsley leaves, finely chopped

For the caper browned butter

50g unsalted butter
1 garlic clove, crushed
20g capers (drained weight)

An easy caper butter and the garlic and parsley butter really make this dish special. It's a simple dish with a serious amount of flavour. If you have someone coming over for dinner one evening, this will go down a storm.

Preheat the oven to 220°C (200°C fan/gas mark 7) and line a baking tray with baking paper.

Put the potatoes in a large saucepan of water and bring to the boil, then cook for 13–15 minutes until tender. Drain in a colander and allow to steam for a few moments, then transfer to a large bowl, season with salt and pepper and keep warm.

Fill the same saucepan with water and add a little salt. Bring to the boil, add the asparagus and broccoli, and cook for 4 minutes. Drain in a colander and transfer to a large bowl. Season with salt and pepper and keep warm.

Meanwhile, place the salmon fillets on the lined baking tray, skin side up. Season with a little salt and pepper, drizzle with olive oil and brush the seasoning over evenly. Bake in the oven for 8–10 minutes, until the fish flakes easily. Remove and keep warm.

To make the garlic and parsley butter, melt the butter in a small saucepan over a medium heat, then add the garlic and cook for 1 minute. Stir in the parsley, then drizzle half the garlic butter over the potatoes and the remaining garlic butter over the greens. Toss each to coat well.

Using the same saucepan (no need to clean it), make the caper butter sauce. Melt the butter over a medium-high heat until it starts to brown and smell nutty. Remove from the heat and add the garlic (it will gently cook in the residual heat) and capers.

Serve the potatoes and greens with the salmon, drizzling the caper browned butter over the salmon. Serve with the lemon wedges or cheeks to squeeze over.

Tip

To air-fry the crumbed fish, cook in the air fryer at 190°C for 11–13 minutes, until golden and crispy.

Crispy Cod with Creamy Bean Mash

SERVES

4

PREP: 15 mins
COOK: 15 mins

For the fish and crumb

90g dried breadcrumbs
30g white sesame seeds
3–4 thyme sprigs, leaves picked
handful of parsley leaves,
  finely chopped
1 tsp garlic powder
½ tsp smoked paprika
2 tbsp olive oil
4 skinless, boneless cod loin
  fillets (about 150g each)
4 tsp Dijon mustard
salt and freshly ground
  black pepper

For the bean mash

1 tbsp olive oil
1 onion, finely chopped
3 garlic cloves, crushed
2 x 400g tins cannellini beans,
  drained and rinsed
100ml vegetable stock
60g crème fraîche
1 tsp Dijon mustard
finely grated zest of 1 lemon
  (preferably unwaxed)
3–4 thyme sprigs, leaves picked
1 tbsp grated Parmesan cheese

For the buttered peas

300g frozen petits pois
15g butter

Adding herbs and spices to a breadcrumb coating is such a great idea. It adds bags of flavour. Instead of the usual mashed potatoes, I've used creamy cannellini beans, which go very well with the crispy fish. Extra plant protein for the win.

Preheat the oven to 220°C (200°C fan/gas mark 7) and place a greased baking rack over a baking tray.

Make the crumb mix by combining the breadcrumbs, sesame seeds, herbs, garlic powder and paprika in a bowl (keeping some parsley back for garnishing). Season with salt and pepper and drizzle in the olive oil. Combine until the mixture resembles wet sand. Spread it out on a large tray.

Season the cod fillets on both sides with a little salt and pepper, then brush the Dijon mustard evenly over them. Place in the tray of crumbs and cover with the crumb mix, gently pressing it into the fillets until evenly coated all over. Carefully place onto the greased rack and bake in the oven for 13–14 minutes until the crumb is golden and the fish cooked through.

Meanwhile, make the bean mash. Heat the oil in a large frying pan over a medium heat, add the onion and cook for 6–7 minutes until soft, translucent and starting to caramelise. Stir in the garlic and cook for another minute until fragrant, then tip in the drained beans and add the stock. Simmer for 1–2 minutes, then remove from the heat and use a potato masher to crush the beans. Stir in the crème fraîche, mustard, lemon zest, thyme and Parmesan. Season and set aside to keep warm. Cut the zested lemon into wedges or cheeks, for serving.

Cook the peas in a saucepan of boiling water for 3–4 minutes, drain, return to the same pan and add the butter, stirring to allow the butter to melt through and coat the peas.

Divide the mash, buttered peas and fish among four warm plates. Scatter with parsley and serve with the lemon wedges or cheeks.

Sea Bass and Snazzy Rice

SERVES

4

PREP: 10 mins
COOK: 20 mins

8 boneless sea bass fillets
   (see Tip)
2 tsp ground cumin
drizzle of olive oil
salt and freshly ground
   black pepper
1 lemon, cut into wedges,
   to serve

For the jewelled rice

100g frozen sweetcorn kernels
2 tbsp olive oil
1 onion, finely chopped
2 garlic cloves, crushed
½ tsp ground cumin
4 x 125g packets of ready-
   cooked basmati rice
100g pomegranate seeds
generous handful of dill fronds,
   finely chopped
generous handful of parsley
   leaves, finely chopped
generous handful of coriander
   leaves, finely chopped
small handful of mint leaves,
   finely chopped
20g flaked almonds, toasted
   (see page 64)

You will love the speed and simplicity of this one. It's a great weeknight dinner after a busy day. The snazzy rice with this one tastes amazing. You don't have to use all the herbs included, but if you do, it takes plain basmati rice to a new level. The toasted almond flakes bring an extra crunch too.

Start by preparing the rice. Cook the corn for the rice in a small saucepan of boiling water for 3–4 minutes until tender. Drain in a sieve and keep warm.

Heat the oil in a large frying pan or wok over a medium heat, add the onion and cook for 5–6 minutes until starting to caramelise. Stir in the garlic and cumin, cook for another minute until fragrant, then tip in the ready-cooked rice along with a small dash of water and gently warm through for a couple of minutes. Season with salt and pepper and keep warm.

Next, cook the fish. Pat the fillets dry with kitchen paper (particularly the skin side, to ensure crisping) and season on all sides with the cumin and some salt and pepper, rubbing it in evenly.

Heat the drizzle of oil in a large, non-stick frying pan over a medium-high heat. You may need to cook the fish in two-three batches, depending on the size of your pan. Add the sea bass, skin side down, and cook for 2 minutes until the skin is golden and crispy, then carefully flip each one over and cook the underside for another 2 minutes (sea bass fillets are pretty thin, so they cook super quick!). Set aside, skin side up, to keep warm.

Just before serving, stir the corn, pomegranate seeds, most of the chopped herbs and the toasted almonds into the warm rice.

Serve the fish over the colourful rice and scatter the remaining herbs over the whole lot. Enjoy with lemon wedges on the side to squeeze over.

Tip

Switch it up and go for a different fish such as monkfish, sea bream or cod, but bear in mind that they may be thicker than sea bass fillets, so might need a longer cooking time.

Coronation-stylie Chicken with Chickpeas

SERVES

4

PREP: 15 mins
COOK: 30 mins, *plus resting*

4 large skinless, boneless chicken breasts (about 680g total)
1 tsp garlic powder
1 tbsp curry powder, plus a pinch
1 tbsp olive oil, plus extra for drizzling
30g flaked almonds
1 onion, finely chopped
2 garlic cloves, crushed
300g baby spinach
1 x 400g tin chickpeas, drained and rinsed
150g dried apricots, finely chopped (or raisins)
150g reduced-fat crème fraîche
2 tsp honey
salt and freshly ground black pepper

This juicy chicken with chickpeas and spinach riffs on those classic coronation chicken flavours and is a real winner. With minimal prep time, you get maximum taste, and it tastes equally as fantastic straight out of the oven as it does cold in a lunchbox the next day.

Preheat the oven to 220°C (200°C fan/gas mark 7) and line a baking tray with baking paper.

Put the chicken breasts on the lined baking tray and season with a little salt and pepper. Sprinkle over the garlic powder and the pinch of curry powder and drizzle with a little olive oil then brush the seasoning over evenly. Bake in the oven for 20–21 minutes, until cooked through. Set aside to rest, covered with foil, for 8–10 minutes. Just before serving, slice it into thick pieces, if desired, or leave as is.

Meanwhile, toast the flaked almonds in a dry frying pan over a medium-high heat for 3–4 minutes until golden. Allow to cool, then roughly chop.

Heat the 1 tablespoon of oil in a large frying pan over a medium heat, add the onion and cook for 3–4 minutes until soft and translucent. Stir in the garlic and cook for another minute until fragrant, then add the 1 tablespoon of curry powder and the spinach, combining well to ensure the spinach wilts and the garlic doesn't burn. Reduce the heat to medium-low and tip in the chickpeas and dried apricots, stirring well to combine and warm through. Just before serving, stir in the crème fraîche and honey, and season with salt and pepper.

Serve the chicken with the spinach and chickpea mix and scatter the toasted almonds over the whole lot.

Tip

To air-fry the chicken, cook at 200°C for 16–18 minutes, until cooked through, before resting and slicing.

Garlic Butter Chicken with Quinoa

SERVES

4

PREP: 10 mins
COOK: 25 mins, *plus resting*

4 large skinless, boneless
chicken breasts (about 680g
total)
1 tsp smoked paprika
1 tsp dried oregano
drizzle of olive oil
salt and freshly ground
black pepper
1 lemon, cut into wedges,
to serve

For the quinoa

400ml chicken stock (made
with 1 stock cube)
200g quinoa, rinsed
1 tsp garlic powder
2–3 thyme sprigs, leaves picked
1 tbsp grated Parmesan cheese
pinch of dried chilli flakes
(optional)

For the greens

1 head broccoli, cut into
even-sized florets
100g curly kale, chopped
1 tbsp olive oil
juice of ½ lemon (about 1 tbsp)
4 tsp grated Parmesan cheese

For the garlic butter

60g butter, roughly diced
4 garlic cloves, crushed

This is another good option for a lunch on the go. Plain quinoa can be a bit boring and bland, but this recipe pimps it up with spices, herbs and cheese and makes it beautiful to eat. The garlic butter drizzled over the chicken is dreamy, too. This one is a winner.

Preheat the oven to 220°C (200°C fan/gas mark 7) and line a baking tray with baking paper.

Put the chicken on the baking tray and sprinkle with the paprika and oregano. Season with salt and pepper, drizzle with a little olive oil and brush the seasoning over evenly. Bake for 20–21 minutes, until cooked through, then rest, covered with foil, for 8–10 minutes. Just before serving, cut into 1–1.5cm-thick slices.

While the chicken is cooking, cook the quinoa. Bring the stock to the boil in a saucepan, add the quinoa, partially cover and simmer over a medium heat for 12–15 minutes until all the stock is absorbed and the pan is dry. Check it regularly: the quinoa is cooked when the grains are translucent and the outer germ separates. Stir in the garlic powder and thyme leaves in the last minute of cooking. Remove from the heat, fluff with a fork and stir in the Parmesan (and chilli flakes, if using). Set aside.

Meanwhile, prepare the greens. Cook the broccoli and kale in a large saucepan of boiling salted water for 4 minutes. Drain well in a colander and let steam for 1–2 minutes, then toss with the oil and lemon juice and season with salt and pepper. Set aside.

For the garlic butter, melt the butter in a small saucepan over a medium-low heat, then add the garlic and cook gently for 2–3 minutes, without letting it colour. Remove from the heat and stir 2 tablespoons of the garlic butter into the quinoa.

Divide the quinoa and greens among four warm plates. Serve the sliced chicken over the quinoa and drizzle the remaining garlic butter over the chicken. Scatter the Parmesan over the greens and enjoy with lemon wedges to squeeze over.

/ EASY PEASY DINNERS

Tip

The 4-herb 'ratatouille' is a cracking side veg option for all sorts of meat or fish, and you'll even see it pop up again in the Fancy-pants Omelette recipe on page 138 if you have any left over.

Golden Crusted Chicken with Ratatouille

SERVES

4

PREP: 15 mins
COOK: 20 mins

For the 4-herb 'ratatouille'

2–3 tbsp olive oil
1 aubergine, cut into 1–2cm dice
1 courgette, cut into 1–2cm dice
2 garlic cloves, crushed
1 tbsp double-concentrated
   tomato puree
100g red peppers (from a jar),
   drained and finely chopped
4–5 thyme sprigs, leaves picked
1 tsp dried oregano
1 x 400g tin chopped tomatoes
2 tsp honey
generous handful of basil
   leaves, thinly sliced
handful of tarragon leaves,
   finely chopped

For the crumbed chicken

4 large skinless, boneless
   chicken breasts
80g plain flour
1 egg, whisked
80g dried breadcrumbs
30g white sesame seeds
1 tsp dried oregano
1 tsp garlic powder
1 tsp smoked paprika
2–3 tbsp olive oil
salt and freshly ground
   black pepper
lemon wedges, to serve

I'm obsessed with breadcrumbing chicken: it goes all crispy when it's cooked and feels like you're eating a giant chicken nugget. The ratatouille is a nice and different way to enjoy your veggies. I've used a few herbs here, but feel free to use fewer if you don't have them all handy. I think you'll really enjoy this one.

Start with the ratatouille, so it can simmer while the chicken cooks. Heat the oil in a large frying pan over a medium-high heat, add the aubergine and courgette and cook for 5–6 minutes, stirring, until starting to soften and caramelise. Add the garlic, tomato puree, red peppers, thyme and oregano, then the chopped tomatoes. Fill the empty tin about a quarter-full with water, swirl it in the tin, and add the water to the pan. Reduce the heat to medium-low and simmer for 8–10 minutes, until the mixture is thick and chunky. Remove from the heat and stir in the honey and herbs. Set aside to keep warm.

Meanwhile, place each chicken breast between two sheets of baking paper and use a meat mallet to flatten the breasts until thin and even in thickness (no thicker than 1cm).

Prepare three shallow bowls, one with the flour, one with the whisked egg and one with the breadcrumbs mixed with the sesame seeds. Mix the oregano, garlic powder, paprika and a little salt into the flour. Lightly dust a chicken breast with the flour, then dip it into the egg, allowing the excess egg to drip off. Gently roll in the crumb mix to coat on all sides and set aside on a large tray lined with baking paper. Repeat, to coat all the chicken.

Heat a drizzle of olive oil in a large frying pan over a medium-high heat and fry two of the crumbed breasts for 2½ minutes on each side, until golden, crispy and cooked through. Drain on a tray lined with kitchen paper. Wipe the pan clean, add another drizzle of olive oil and fry the remaining chicken. Set aside.

Serve the chicken with the ratatouille and lemon wedges.

Get Your Chops Round This

SERVES

4

PREP: 15 mins
COOK: 25 mins

4 pork chops (about 1.2kg total)
1 tsp dried sage
1 tsp garlic powder
drizzle of olive oil
salt and freshly ground
 black pepper

For the quick-pickled red onion

¼ red onion, very thinly sliced
3 tbsp red wine vinegar

For the mash

3–4 floury potatoes, like Maris
 Piper (about 600g peeled
 weight), peeled and cut into
 2cm dice
2 tsp Dijon mustard
60g crème fraîche

For the buttered beans -and-greens

200ml chicken stock (made
 with ½ stock cube)
10g butter
1 x 400g tin cannellini beans,
 drained and rinsed
150g frozen petits pois
50g wild rocket

Comfort food at its best. If you haven't cooked pork chops in a while, give this recipe a go. The creamy mash alongside the buttered beans and greens is spot on. It makes a wonderful family lunch on a Sunday afternoon. Enjoy.

Lay out the thin slices of red onion in a large shallow bowl. Drizzle over the vinegar, toss to coat and leave to pickle for 20–25 minutes. Stir every now and again to ensure even pickling.

Meanwhile, make the mash. Put the diced potatoes in a large saucepan of water and bring to the boil, then cook for about 25 minutes until tender. Drain in a colander, then transfer to a large bowl (or the same pan used to cook them, off the heat) and use a potato masher to mash well. If you prefer a smooth mash, push the mixture through a potato ricer. Stir in the Dijon mustard and crème fraîche and season with salt and pepper. Set aside to keep warm.

At the same time, cook the pork chops and the buttered greens. Sprinkle the pork chops with the dried sage and garlic powder and season with salt and pepper. Drizzle over a little olive oil and brush to evenly coat. Heat a large frying pan over a medium-high heat, then cook the chops for 4–5 minutes on each side. Keep warm.

For the buttered greens, heat the chicken stock in a large saucepan or frying pan over a high heat (if you use the same pan you used to cook the pork, you'll get some added flavour from the caramelised bits that may have stuck). Bring to the boil and simmer for 2–3 minutes until it has reduced by half. Reduce the heat to low, add the butter, beans and peas, and cook for 2–3 minutes. Remove the pan from the heat and tip in all the rocket, stirring well to wilt.

Serve the buttered greens (and pan juices) with the pork chops on top, and the mash alongside. Drain the red onion and scatter it over the pork for a delicious, acidic bite with every forkful. Season with more salt and pepper, if needed.

Tip

To air-fry the seasoned pork chops, cook in the air fryer at 200°C for 14–15 minutes, flipping them halfway through.

Cheesy Mash-topped Beef Pie

SERVES

4

swap the Worcestershire sauce for Henderson's relish

PREP: 15 mins *(see Tip)*
COOK: 45 mins

1 tbsp olive oil
1 onion, finely chopped
750g minced beef
200g chestnut mushrooms, finely chopped
2 garlic cloves, crushed
1 tsp cayenne pepper (or more if you like it spicy)
2 tsp dried mixed Italian herbs
2 tbsp red wine vinegar
200g tinned chopped tomatoes
1½ tbsp Worcestershire sauce
130g frozen petits pois
120g frozen sweetcorn kernels
salt and freshly ground black pepper
handful of parsley leaves, chopped, to serve (optional)

For the cheesy mash topping

1kg floury potatoes like Maris Piper, peeled and cut into small 2cm dice
80g cream cheese
120g extra-mature cheddar cheese, grated

This is a weekly favourite in our house – it's such a hearty and comforting meal. You can throw in literally any leftover veg you have in the fridge, so feel free to switch it up or swap the veg out. This keeps well in the fridge for a couple of days too, if you'd like to make it and have the leftovers the next day.

Preheat the oven to 220°C (200°C fan/gas mark 7) and have a deep baking or roasting dish ready (like a lasagne dish).

Start with the mash, since that will take the longest. Put the diced potatoes in a large saucepan of water and bring to the boil, then cook for about 25 minutes until tender. Drain in a colander, then transfer to a large bowl (or the same pan used to cook them, off the heat). Add the cream cheese, season with salt and pepper and use a potato masher to mash the potatoes well. Stir in half the grated cheddar until melted, then set aside and keep warm.

Meanwhile, make the beefy filling. Heat the oil in a large frying pan over a medium heat, add the onion and cook for 3–4 minutes until soft and translucent. Tip in all the mince, increase the heat to high and fry for 3–5 minutes until browned, using a wooden spoon to break up the mince as it cooks. Add the mushrooms, garlic, cayenne pepper and dried herbs and cook, stirring continuously, for 4–5 minutes, then add the red wine vinegar, chopped tomatoes, Worcestershire sauce, peas and corn. Cook, stirring regularly, for another 1–3 minutes, or until the mixture is free of excess moisture. Season with salt and pepper, then tip into the baking dish.

Spread the warm mash over the mince and scatter over the remaining cheddar. Bake in the oven for 17–20 minutes, or until the cheese is golden and bubbling.

Scatter over the parsley (if using) and serve with a green salad on the side, if desired.

Tip

Shop-bought mash is a handy shortcut. It might not have that made-from-scratch freshness, but it'll save time. Just heat it through, stir in the cheeses and then season.

Fully Loaded Jacket Potatoes

SERVES

4

swap the
Worcestershire
sauce for
Henderson's
relish

This has everything you could possibly want in a high-protein dinner. The crispy baked potato with butter and cheese is delicious with the spicy beef and bean chilli on top. I like to make a double batch of the chilli for the following day. It tastes amazing on rice, pasta or even a slice of toast.

PREP: 10 mins
COOK: 1+ hours

4 medium baking potatoes
drizzle of olive oil
salt and freshly ground
   black pepper

For the beef and bean chilli

1 tbsp olive oil
1 onion, finely chopped
2 garlic cloves, crushed
500g 5%-fat minced beef
1 tbsp ground cumin
1 tsp ground coriander
1 tsp chilli powder (or to taste)
250ml beef stock (made with
   ½ stock cube)
1 x 400g tin chopped tomatoes
1 x 400g tin kidney beans,
   drained and rinsed
1 tbsp double-concentrated
   tomato puree
2 tsp Worcestershire sauce

To serve

50g extra-mature cheddar
   cheese, grated
85g soured cream
1 red chilli, thinly sliced
   (deseeded if preferred)
handful of parsley or coriander
   leaves, chopped

Preheat the oven to 200°C (180°C fan/gas mark 6) and line a baking tray with baking paper.

Brush the potatoes all over with olive oil and season with salt. Place on the lined tray and bake for 50–70 minutes (depending on their size), or until the skins are crispy and the flesh is soft. Pierce the centre of your largest spud with the tip of a sharp knife: the potato should be tender.

In the last 30 minutes of the potatoes' baking, start to prepare the beef and bean chilli. Heat the oil in a large frying pan over a medium heat, add the onion and cook for 3–4 minutes until soft and translucent. Stir in the garlic, cook for another minute until fragrant, then turn up the heat to high. Add the minced beef, cumin, coriander and chilli powder, then cook for 4–5 minutes until the meat is browned, using a wooden spoon to break the mince up as it cooks. Add the beef stock, chopped tomatoes, kidney beans, tomato puree and Worcestershire sauce and, once bubbling, reduce the heat to medium and simmer for 20–30 minutes, stirring occasionally, until the mixture is thick and chunky and there is no excess moisture in the pan. Remove the pan from the heat and season the mixture with salt and pepper.

To serve, carefully cut a deep criss-cross into each hot potato and press the sides in to open and squeeze out some of the potato flesh. Season lightly with salt and pepper, then place on four plates. Generously divide the chilli mix over and around the potatoes and top with the grated cheese, along with a dollop of soured cream. Finish with the chilli and parsley (or coriander).

EASY PEASY DINNERS

Sticky Steak Stir-fry with Crushed Potatoes

SERVES

4

swap the soy sauce for tamari

Stir-fries never let you down. They're quick to prep, easy to cook, and you can't go wrong with this one. The simple sauce is so easy to make and it beats any ultra-processed sauce you get in a packet or jar. Once you invest in the four sauce ingredients, you'll be making it time and time again.

PREP: 15 mins
COOK: 15 mins

750g baby potatoes, halved or larger ones quartered to ensure even cooking
2 tbsp olive oil
4 spring onions, trimmed and thinly sliced
3 garlic cloves, crushed
30g fresh ginger, finely grated
2 tsp white sesame seeds
handful of coriander leaves, chopped (optional)
1 red chilli, thinly sliced (deseeded if preferred)
salt and freshly ground black pepper
1 lime, cut into cheeks, to serve

For the sauce
2 tbsp mirin
2 tbsp rice wine vinegar
3 tbsp soy sauce
1 tbsp honey

For the steak and mangetout
4 sirloin steaks, visible fat removed (or 700g shop-bought beef stir-fry strips)
2 tbsp olive oil, plus extra for drizzling
150g mangetout

Remove the steaks from the fridge 30 minutes before cooking and cut into 1cm-thick strips (if not using pre-sliced meat).

Put the potatoes in a large saucepan of water and bring to the boil, then simmer for 14–15 minutes until tender. Drain in a colander and allow to steam.

Heat the olive oil in the same saucepan over a low heat, add the spring onions, along with most of the garlic and ginger, and stir-fry for 45–60 seconds, then tip the drained potatoes back in. Use the back of a fork to lightly crush each potato. Season with a little salt and pepper, tossing well to combine the potatoes with the fragrant oily mixture. Set aside to keep warm.

Make the sauce by whisking together the ingredients in a bowl.

To cook the steak, heat 1 tablespoon of the oil in a large frying pan or wok over a high heat. Add half the steak and cook for 2–3 minutes, stirring until browned on all sides. Transfer to a large bowl and cook the remaining steak in the residual oil in the pan. Transfer the second batch to the bowl.

Using the same pan (off the heat, as it will still be very hot), add a small drizzle of oil along with the remaining garlic and ginger. Stir for 30 seconds to gently cook, then add the sauce and mangetout. Simmer over a medium-high heat for 2–3 minutes until thickened, then reduce the heat to low and return the steak to the pan (along with any juices from the bowl). Simmer for 1 minute, allowing the sauce to coat the steak. Remove from the heat.

Serve the potatoes with the beef and mangetout. Scatter with sesame seeds, coriander (if using) and chilli, with lime to squeeze over.

Dukkah-coated Steak with Corn

SERVES

4

PREP: 15 mins
COOK: 15 mins, *plus resting*

For the steaks

4 sirloin steaks, visible fat removed
2 tbsp olive oil, plus extra for brushing
25g shop-bought dukkah

For the corn

8 corn on the cob halves
50g butter
2 garlic cloves, crushed
½ tsp smoked paprika
¼ tsp dried chilli flakes
finely grated zest of 1 lime (preferably unwaxed)
30g Manchego or gruyère cheese, finely grated
salt and freshly ground black pepper

You may have never come across dukkah before, but it's a brilliant spice blend that you shouldn't miss, so I'll try my best to describe it. It's a Middle Eastern and Egyptian spice mix, usually made with toasted nuts, seeds and spices like coriander, cumin and sesame seeds. It has a warm, nutty and slightly spicy flavour, with a hint of saltiness, and it really gives this steak so much flavour. It's a nice change from using peppercorn sauce or tomato ketchup.

Remove the steaks from the fridge 30 minutes before cooking.

To cook the steaks, heat the oil in a large frying pan over a high heat. Once hot, add the steaks, cooking for 2 minutes on each side (for medium) or 45–60 seconds longer on each side for thicker cuts, or longer if you prefer your steaks more well-done. You may need to cook two steaks at a time to avoid overcrowding the pan. Set the steaks aside on a clean chopping board, cover with foil, and leave to rest for 8–10 minutes before slicing.

While the steaks are resting, bring a large saucepan of salted water to the boil, add the corn on the cob and cook for 7–8 minutes until tender. Drain well in a colander and leave for a few minutes to steam. Season with salt and pepper.

While the corn cooks, melt the butter in a small saucepan over a medium-low heat. Add the garlic, smoked paprika and chilli flakes, then remove the pan from the heat and add the lime zest. Pour the butter over the cooked corn, tossing well to evenly coat. Cut the zested lime into wedges.

Brush the sliced steak lightly with olive oil, season with pepper, then scatter over the dukkah.

Divide the dukkah-coated steak slices among four warm plates and serve the buttered corn alongside. Scatter the Manchego (or gruyère) cheese over the warm corn to melt and serve with the lime wedges alongside to squeeze over the whole lot.

Tip

To cook this on the barbecue, cook the corn as opposite, drain and brush with a little olive oil, finishing it on the barbecue. Barbecue your steaks too, until done to your liking.

Steak with Parmesan Mash

SERVES

4

PREP: 15 mins
COOK: 30 mins, *plus resting*

For the Parmesan mash

3–4 floury potatoes, like Maris
    Piper (about 600g peeled
    weight), peeled and cut into
    2cm dice
2–3 tbsp milk (if needed)
50g finely grated Parmesan
    cheese
60g reduced-fat crème fraîche
salt and freshly ground
    black pepper

For the garlic butter cabbage wedges

2 pointed (spring/sweetheart)
    cabbages, tougher outer
    leaves removed
olive oil, for drizzling
40g unsalted butter, softened
2 garlic cloves, crushed

For the steaks

4 ribeye steaks (or any that fit
    your budget; around 200g
    each), removed from the
    fridge about 30 minutes
    before cooking
generous pinch of dried
    oregano
drizzle of olive oil

Mashed potato with Parmesan cheese and crème fraîche is absolutely top tier. It doesn't get better than this with the charred cabbage either. This is one of my favourite post-workout meals – it's got the perfect mix of protein and carbohydrates to refuel after lifting weights.

Start with the mash. Put the diced potatoes in a large saucepan of water and bring to the boil, then cook for about 25 minutes until tender. Drain in a colander, transfer to a large bowl (or the same pan used to cook them, off the heat) and use a potato masher to mash well (or push them through a potato ricer if you prefer a smooth mash). If needed, add a splash of milk. Stir in the grated Parmesan and crème fraîche to melt through and season generously with salt and pepper. Keep warm.

Meanwhile, preheat the oven to 220°C (200°C fan/gas mark 7) and line a large baking tray with baking paper. Cut the cabbages lengthways through the core to make eight 4–5cm-thick wedges. Spread them out on the baking tray, drizzle generously with olive oil, season with salt and pepper and roast for 16 minutes, rotating halfway. Meanwhile, mix the butter with the garlic in a bowl and season with salt and pepper.

After 16 minutes roasting, remove the tray of cabbage from the oven and turn the oven temperature down to 190°C (170°C fan/gas mark 5). Generously brush or dollop the softened garlic butter over the wedges, ensuring they are evenly covered. Return to the oven for a maximum of 4 minutes (any longer and the garlic will burn), then remove and set aside to keep warm.

Season the steaks with salt, pepper and a pinch of oregano on both sides. Heat the oil in a large frying pan over a high heat. Add the steaks and cook for 2 minutes on each side (for medium), adding an extra 45–60 seconds on each side for thicker cuts, or longer if you prefer them well-done – cook in batches, if necessary. Set them aside on a clean board, covered with foil, to rest for 8–10 minutes before slicing. Serve the Parmesan mash and steak with the garlic butter cabbage wedges alongside.

Tip

Got some leftover cabbage? Don't chuck it! Thinly slice it and toss it into salads for a bit of crunch or add it to stir-fries and slow-cooks for a handy veg and fibre boost.

Moroccan-style Lamb and Butternut Squash

SERVES

4

PREP: 10 mins
COOK: 30 mins

12 lamb chops, fat trimmed
500g peeled and diced
   butternut squash, cut
   into 2cm pieces
2 tbsp olive oil
2 tsp ground cinnamon
2 tsp ground cumin
2 tsp ground coriander
1 tsp dried chilli flakes
salt and freshly ground
   black pepper

For the couscous

2 tbsp olive oil
1 onion, thinly sliced
2 garlic cloves, crushed
250g couscous
500ml boiling-hot chicken
   stock (made with
   1 stock cube)
handful of mint leaves
handful of coriander leaves

To finish

30g feta cheese, crumbled
15g flaked almonds, toasted
   (see page 64)

This is a proper crowd-pleaser, with unbelievable levels of flavour from the flaked almonds and crumbled feta cheese. It's all these little extra touches that really make this a standout dish for me. Friends and family will be well impressed if you make the effort with this.

Preheat the oven to 200°C (180°C fan/gas mark 6) and line your largest baking tray with baking paper (or two smaller trays if your largest can't fit everything in a single layer).

Put the lamb chops, squash, olive oil, cinnamon, cumin, coriander and chilli flakes into a large bowl. Season with salt and pepper, then massage the spices into the whole lot with clean hands.

Spread out the spiced lamb and squash evenly on the large tray and roast in the oven for 26–30 minutes until the lamb is cooked and the squash is tender.

Meanwhile, prepare the couscous base. Heat the oil in a frying pan over a medium heat, add the onion and cook for 4–5 minutes, then reduce the heat to low and cook for 15–20 minutes until the onion deeply caramelises and turns golden. Keep an eye on it, stirring occasionally: you may need to reduce the heat to avoid the onion burning. Stir in the garlic in the last 2–3 minutes. Season with salt and pepper.

At the same time, make the couscous. Put the couscous in a large heatproof bowl and pour over the hot stock. Cover and leave for 10 minutes, then fluff with a fork. Stir in the caramelised onion and garlic mix. Thinly slice most of the mint and coriander leaves and stir in (setting aside some whole leaves to garnish).

Spread the couscous out on a large, warm serving platter and place the lamb and squash on top of the couscous. Drizzle the delicious juices in the roasting tray over the whole lot.

Sprinkle with the crumbled feta, toasted almonds and the remaining herbs and serve.

Tip

To air-fry the seasoned lamb chops, cook in the air fryer at 190°C for about 12 minutes until tender and the fat has rendered and becomes nice and crispy.

Easy Peasy Duck Pancakes

SERVES

4

PREP: 10 mins
COOK: 35–45 mins, *plus resting*

4 extra-large duck breasts
300ml fresh chicken stock (or
  made ½ stock cube)
2 tsp honey
2 tsp Chinese 5-spice
salt and freshly ground
  black pepper

For the pancakes *(makes
16 pancakes, 4 per serving)*

300g plain flour, plus extra
  for dusting
generous pinch of salt
olive oil

To serve

3–4 tbsp hoisin sauce
2–3 baby cucumbers, trimmed
  and sliced into very thin strips
4–5 spring onions, trimmed,
  halved widthways, then sliced
  lengthways into thin strips

This feels like a real treat. I rarely cook with duck, but this dish is well worth the effort and it tastes unreal. Next time you feel like ordering a Chinese takeaway, give this a try instead. Knowing you've made your very own pancakes too makes you enjoy it even more when it all comes together and you roll them up.

Preheat the oven to 180°C (160°C fan/gas mark 4).

Lightly score the skin of each duck breast with a sharp knife. Place them skin side down in a large frying pan over a medium heat and let the fat render for 15 minutes: there will eventually be plenty of liquid fat in the pan. Increase the heat to high and fry for 1–2 minutes, to allow the skin to crisp up. Turn the duck breasts over and cook the underside for 1 minute.

Use tongs to transfer the breasts into a deep, medium baking dish, skin side up. (Discard the rendered duck fat in the pan.) Pour the chicken stock and honey into the dish, taking care not to splash it onto the skin. Sprinkle the breasts with the 5-spice and season with salt and pepper. Cook in the oven for 15–25 minutes, depending on how well done you like your duck.

Remove from the oven and from the dish and rest for 10–15 minutes while you make the pancakes. Do not cover, to ensure the skin remains crispy. Use a very sharp knife to thinly slice the breasts before serving.

To make the pancakes, sift the flour into a large bowl and add the salt. Add 220ml hot water and combine until the mixture comes together to form a dough (you may need to add more flour if the dough is too sticky). Tip the dough out onto a clean, floured work surface and knead for 8–10 minutes until smooth and elastic, sprinkling with more flour if the dough still seems too sticky.

Tip

Make this meat-free: fry finely chopped mushrooms until caramelised, add crushed garlic and fry briefly, add a drained 400g tin of black beans. Warm through, mix in hoisin sauce.

Pull off pieces of dough, about 25g each, and shape into small round balls (about 16).

Use a floured rolling pin to roll each ball into a very thin, flat disc on a sheet of baking paper. They don't need to be perfectly round, just as thin as possible. Set each pancake aside, keeping them separate with little squares of baking paper to prevent sticking. If you're making them ahead of time, cover completely and place in the fridge until ready to cook, so they don't dry out.

Cook the pancakes in batches: lightly brush a large, non-stick frying pan with a little olive oil and place over a high heat. Set your timer and cook each pancake for no longer than 20–21 seconds, before flipping and cooking for another 20–21 seconds. A few golden blisters are great, but avoid burnt spots. Transfer to a large tray lined with kitchen paper to absorb excess grease. Brush the pan with more oil between cooking each pancake.

Let everyone assemble their own pancakes or prepare them ready to eat. Put some duck slices into the centre of each pancake and add hoisin sauce, cucumber strips and spring onion strips.

PASTA &
NOODLE
WINNERS

Three Cheese Pasta Salad

SERVES

4

swap the
Parmesan for
vegetarian
Italian hard
cheese

PREP: 15 mins
COOK: 15 mins

300g high-protein pasta (any
   shape)
2 tbsp olive oil, plus extra for
   drizzling
25g pine nuts
400g cherry tomatoes, halved
250g mini mozzarella balls (also
   called pearls) or roughly torn
   fresh mozzarella (drained
   weight)
60g feta cheese, crumbled
2 tbsp finely grated Parmesan
   cheese, plus extra to serve
very generous handful of basil
   leaves (optional)
80g wild rocket
salt and freshly ground
   black pepper

Fresh, feel-good food. This is an awesome one to take to work, or to have as a sharing salad at a barbecue with friends. It works with any shape of pasta and keeps well in the fridge for a couple of days.

Cook the pasta according to the packet instructions (usually in a saucepan of salted boiling water for 8–12 minutes, depending on the shape and type). Drain and rinse under cold running water. Toss with a drizzle of olive oil to prevent sticking, and leave to cool.

Meanwhile, toast the pine nuts in a dry frying pan over a medium-high heat for 3–4 minutes until golden, shaking the pan occasionally, then remove from the pan and set aside.

Combine the cooked pasta, tomatoes, mozzarella, feta, 2 tablespoons of olive oil and the Parmesan in a large bowl. Season with salt and pepper. Just before serving, tear or slice the basil (if using) and stir into the salad to combine. Serve with the wild rocket and finish with a scattering of pine nuts and Parmesan.

Enjoy immediately or store the salad in the fridge in an airtight container for up to 2–3 days, keeping the basil, rocket and pine nuts separately and adding them just before serving to ensure the greens don't blacken or wilt and the pine nuts keep their crunch.

Tip

Never keep fresh basil in the fridge – store it at room temperature. Slice, chop or tear it just before adding it to your dish for the best flavour.

Mushroom and Chickpea Stroganoff

SERVES

4

PREP: 15 mins
COOK: 20 mins

2 tbsp olive oil, plus extra for drizzling
1 onion, finely chopped
3 garlic cloves, crushed
500g mixed mushrooms (such as portobello, chestnut, oyster), roughly chopped
1 tsp smoked paprika
1 tsp dried thyme
juice of ½ lemon (about 1 tbsp)
1 x 400g tin chickpeas, drained and rinsed
150ml vegetable stock
2 tbsp low-sodium soy sauce
1 tsp Dijon mustard
130g reduced-fat crème fraîche
300g high-protein spaghetti or tagliatelle
salt and freshly ground black pepper

To serve

50g walnuts, toasted and chopped (see page 42)
generous handful of parsley leaves, chopped

This is a great veggie option, loaded with flavour and protein. The sauce is deliciously creamy and works brilliantly with the mixed mushrooms. The toasted walnuts add a nice crunch and an extra kick of protein so don't forget to add those at the end.

Heat half the oil in a large frying pan over a medium heat, add the onion and cook for 3–4 minutes until soft and translucent. Add the remaining oil and stir in the garlic, mushrooms, smoked paprika and thyme. Turn up the heat to medium-high and cook, stirring regularly, for 6–7 minutes until the mushrooms are golden and tender and the pan starts to look dry.

Add the lemon juice, followed by the chickpeas, vegetable stock, soy sauce and mustard. Combine well and simmer for 3–4 minutes or until the mixture is thick and chunky, and free of excess moisture.

Remove the pan from the heat and stir in the crème fraîche. Season with salt and generous cracks of black pepper.

Meanwhile, cook the pasta according to the packet instructions (usually in a saucepan of salted boiling water for 8–12 minutes). Drain well, then immediately toss in a little olive oil to prevent sticking and season with salt.

Divide the pasta among four warm bowls and spoon over the creamy mushroom and chickpea mixture. Scatter over the toasted walnuts and parsley before tucking in.

PROTEIN _BOOST_

Scatter with your toasted nuts of choice, for crunch.

Hot-smoked Salmon and Broad Bean Pasta

SERVES

4

PREP: 15 mins
COOK: 15 mins

300g high-protein pasta (any shape)

3 tbsp olive oil, plus extra for drizzling

300g podded broad beans (defrosted if using frozen)

juice and finely grated zest of 2 lemons (preferably unwaxed)

40g pitted black olives, sliced

very generous handful of dill fronds, chopped

4 hot-smoked salmon fillets (about 360g in total)

salt and freshly ground black pepper

1 lemon, cut into wedges, to serve

Another brilliant idea for meal prepping. This is Rosie's favourite lunch, and it goes down equally well whether you enjoy it hot or cold. The more you can get into prepping simple things like this for the next day, the easier it is to avoid ultra-processed foods. That's winning.

Cook the pasta according to the packet instructions (usually in a saucepan of salted boiling water for 8–12 minutes, depending on the shape and type). Drain and drizzle with a little olive oil, tossing well to combine and prevent sticking.

Meanwhile, cook the broad beans in a small saucepan of boiling water for 5 minutes. Drain in a colander. Use a sharp knife to snip open the tough skins and gently pinch out and reserve each bright green bean into a bowl, discarding the skins. You should yield around 210g of shelled beans.

Combine the warm pasta, broad beans, 3 tablespoons of olive oil, lemon juice and zest, olives and dill in a large bowl. Season with salt and pepper, then flake the hot-smoked salmon into the bowl. Toss gently to combine, then serve with lemon wedges to squeeze over.

Tip

If hot-smoked salmon fillets are unavailable, you can substitute smoked trout or smoked mackerel fillets. It's the flavour of smoked fish that makes this dish so delightful!

Thai-style Seafood Broth with Egg Noodles

SERVES

4

PREP: 10 mins
COOK: 10 mins, *plus infusing*

1 tbsp olive oil
200g pak choy, thinly sliced
2 tbsp fish sauce
1 tbsp soy sauce
2 tbsp tamarind paste
juice of 2 limes (about 1 tbsp)
450g raw, shelled king prawns, defrosted if frozen
250g skinless white fish fillets, defrosted if using frozen, cut into 2cm chunks
4 nests of dried egg noodles
generous handful of coriander leaves, to serve

For the broth infusion

1.25 litres fish stock (made with 2½ fish stock cubes or pots)
4 garlic cloves (no need to peel), smashed with the back of a knife
30g fresh ginger (no need to peel), roughly sliced
2 lemongrass stalks, halved lengthways and smashed once or twice with a pestle
3 fresh lime leaves (or 2 dried)
1 large red chilli, halved lengthways, plus extra thinly sliced chilli to serve

If you love hot, spicy and sour food, then this one is for you. It's super easy and quick to prep and has so many wonderful flavours going on. I love the fresh ginger, chilli and lemongrass – they bring out the really authentic fragrant characteristics of well-made Thai food.

Start with the broth, as it needs time to infuse. Pour the fish stock into a large saucepan, add the garlic, ginger, lemongrass, lime leaves and chilli, then bring to a rapid boil for 2 minutes. Remove the pan completely from the heat and set aside for 10 minutes to infuse.

While the broth infuses, heat the olive oil in a large high-sided frying pan or wok over a medium-high heat, add the sliced pak choy and cook, stirring constantly, for 2–3 minutes until slightly softened.

Strain the infused broth through a sieve directly into the pan of pak choy, discarding the contents of the sieve. Stir the fish sauce, soy sauce, tamarind paste and lime juice into the pan. When it simmers, turn the heat down to medium and tip in all the prawns and fish chunks. Poach gently for 5–6 minutes until the fish has cooked through and the prawns are pink. Stir occasionally to ensure everything cooks evenly.

In the last 4–5 minutes, cook the egg noodles according to the packet instructions (usually placing the nests in a large heatproof bowl, pouring over boiling-hot kettle water and leaving for 4–5 minutes, or cooking in a saucepan of simmering water for about 4 minutes: check packaging as brands differ).

Drain the noodles and divide among four bowls. Ladle over the broth and seafood and top with the coriander and sliced chilli.

Tip

Any skinless and deboned white fish will work well here: try cod, hake or unsmoked haddock. Use whichever suits your budget.

Lemon, Garlic and Prawn Stir-fry

SERVES

4

PREP: 15 mins
COOK: 15 mins

600g raw, shelled king prawns, defrosted if frozen
finely grated zest of 3 lemons (preferably unwaxed)
4 garlic cloves, crushed
3 tbsp low-sodium soy sauce
2 tsp honey
2 tsp rice wine vinegar
1 tsp dried chilli flakes, plus extra to serve
½ tsp smoked paprika
2–3 tbsp olive oil
1 red pepper, deseeded and thinly sliced
180g Tenderstem® broccoli (long-stem/broccolini), cut into thirds
2 spring onions, trimmed and thinly sliced
600g fresh egg noodles (see Tip)
salt and freshly ground black pepper
4 tsp white sesame seeds, to serve (optional)

I'm back with another stunning stir-fry here. This one has a lemony zing and garlicky kick to round it off. The method of stir-frying things separately ensures the veggies stay crisp, the prawns stay juicy and the noodles soak up all the lovely sauce. It all happens in one pan, so it's super simple. Enjoy.

Put the prawns in a bowl and add two-thirds of the lemon zest. Season with salt and pepper, toss and set aside.

Halve the zested lemons and squeeze the juice into a second, smaller bowl. Mix in the garlic, soy sauce, honey, rice wine vinegar, chilli flakes and paprika. Set aside.

To cook the veg, heat a drizzle of the oil in a large frying pan or wok over a medium-high heat, add the pepper, broccoli pieces and spring onions and stir-fry for 2–3 minutes, until they are starting to caramelise and soften but still retain their crunch. Transfer the vegetables to a large bowl and set aside.

Add another drizzle of oil to the same pan over a medium-high heat, add half the seasoned prawns and cook for 2–3 minutes until pink and opaque all over. Transfer the cooked prawns to a large bowl and add the remaining lemon zest, then cook the remaining prawns as above and put them in the same bowl (batch-cooking them avoids overcrowding the pan: you want caramelisation on the prawns). Toss to combine and set aside (don't discard the third zested lemon).

Add the sauce mix to the same pan over a medium heat and let it deglaze the pan for about 1 minute, loosening any stuck caramelised bits. Return the vegetables to the pan and let the sauce bubble for about 1 minute until thickened – don't let the garlic burn. Return the cooked prawns to the pan (along with any juices from the bowl) and tip in the egg noodles. Toss for 1–2 minutes until the sauce coats the whole lot and the noodles are warmed through. Remove from the heat and squeeze over the juice of the third zested lemon. Add extra chilli flakes and stir well. Divide among four warm bowls, scattered with sesame seeds (if using).

Tip

Can't find fresh egg noodles? No stress. Just cook 4 nests of dried egg noodles (65–70g per nest) following the method on page 96, then drain them well before adding to the pan.

Extra-easy Chicken Ramen

SERVES

4

PREP: 15 mins
COOK: 15 mins, *not including the slow-cooked chicken*

1 tbsp olive oil
2 garlic cloves, crushed
20g fresh ginger, finely grated
1 litre best-quality chicken stock
4 tbsp low-sodium soy sauce
1 tbsp rice wine vinegar
2 tbsp sweet chilli sauce
400g shredded slow-cooked chicken (see page 184) or succulent cooked and sliced chicken breasts
4 eggs
4 nests of dried egg noodles
1 carrot, peeled and cut into thin, matchstick-size pieces
4 spring onions, trimmed and thinly sliced
salt and freshly ground black pepper

If you've eaten ramen at a restaurant before but never had the courage to make it at home, you must try this. It comes together in a flash and has all the flavours and textures you would expect from a good ramen restaurant. I use slow-cooked chicken here (see page 184), but it also works well with pre-cooked chicken breast.

Heat the oil in a large saucepan over a medium heat. Add the garlic and ginger and cook for 3–4 minutes until softened, then add the chicken stock, soy sauce, rice wine vinegar and sweet chilli sauce. Bring to a simmer, then turn the heat down to low. Cover the pan partially with a lid and simmer gently for 5–6 minutes to allow the flavours to infuse.

Add the shredded chicken in the last minute to gently warm it through. Season with black pepper.

Meanwhile, boil the eggs (5–6 minutes for soft yolks; 8–10 minutes for set yolks), then transfer to a bowl of cold water. Once cooled, peel and slice each one in half. Season with salt and pepper, if desired.

At the same time, prepare the egg noodles according to the packet instructions (usually placing the nests in a large heatproof bowl, pouring over boiling-hot kettle water and leaving for 4–5 minutes, or cooking in a saucepan of simmering water for about 4 minutes: check packaging as brands differ).

Drain the noodles and divide evenly among four warm bowls, ladle over equal amounts of chicken broth and top with the carrot, spring onions and boiled egg halves. Crack over some more pepper before serving, if you like.

Chicken and Pesto Pasta with Tomatoes

SERVES

4

PREP: 10 mins
COOK: 25 mins, *plus resting*

4 large skinless, boneless
   chicken breasts (about 680g
   in total)
½ tsp garlic powder
½ tsp ground paprika
pinch of dried oregano
olive oil, for drizzling
25g pine nuts
250g dried tagliatelle
   (preferably high protein)
80–90g shop-bought basil
   (green) pesto
45g sun-dried tomatoes,
   drained and finely chopped
salt and freshly ground
   black pepper
handful of basil leaves, to serve

This is one of those weeknight meals I have on repeat. My kids love anything pasta and this is by far their favourite. The chicken breast becomes tender and juicy in the oven and the pesto and sun-dried tomatoes add bags of flavour. The toasted pine nuts are not essential but do give it a beautiful crunch on top.

Preheat the oven to 220°C (200°C fan/gas mark 7) and line a baking tray with baking paper.

Put the chicken breasts on the lined baking tray and season with salt and pepper. Sprinkle over the garlic powder, paprika and oregano, drizzle with a little olive oil, and brush the seasoning over evenly. Bake in the oven for 20–21 minutes, until cooked through. Set aside to rest, covered with foil, for 8–10 minutes. Just before serving, slice into 1–1.5cm-thick pieces.

Meanwhile, toast the pine nuts in a dry frying pan over a medium-high heat for 3–4 minutes until golden, shaking the pan occasionally. Remove from the pan and set aside.

At the same time, cook the tagliatelle according to the packet instructions (usually in a saucepan of salted boiling water for 8–12 minutes). Drain the cooked pasta in a colander, then immediately transfer to a large bowl. Add the pesto and sun-dried tomatoes and toss well until the pasta is evenly coated.

Divide the pasta and sliced chicken among four warm plates or bowls. Drizzle with a little more olive oil, then scatter over the toasted pine nuts and fresh basil just before serving.

Tip

To air-fry the seasoned chicken, cook in the air fryer at 220°C for 16–18 minutes until cooked through, before resting and slicing.

Chicken Marsala Pasta with Mushrooms

SERVES

4

PREP: 10 mins
COOK: 30 mins

2–3 tbsp olive oil, plus extra for drizzling

4 large skinless, boneless chicken breasts, or 8 large skinless, boneless chicken thighs (about 800g), cut into 1–1.5cm strips

350g chestnut mushrooms, thinly sliced

2 garlic cloves, crushed

2–3 thyme sprigs, leaves picked, plus extra to garnish

180ml dry (secco) marsala or dry sherry (or just use dry white wine)

100g crème fraîche

300g high-protein spaghetti or tagliatelle

4 tsp finely grated Parmesan cheese

salt and freshly ground black pepper

handful of curly parsley leaves, chopped, to serve

Marsala is a fortified wine, originally from Sicily, known for its rich flavour and versatility in cooking. If you've never cooked with it before, don't worry – it's great. It delivers such a rich flavour with the chicken and mushrooms. Be brave, give this one a go and break away from the traditional pasta sauces. I'm confident you'll be making this one again and again.

Heat 1 tablespoon of the oil in a large frying pan over a high heat, add half the chicken and cook for 4–5 minutes until golden brown on all sides. Remove from the pan, set aside in a bowl and repeat with the remaining chicken, adding a drizzle more oil. (Cooking it in batches avoids overcrowding the pan.) Season the chicken with salt and pepper and set aside.

Put the same pan back over a medium-high heat and add another drizzle of oil. Tip in the mushrooms and cook for 3–5 minutes, stirring regularly, until golden and caramelised. Add the garlic and thyme in the last minute, then immediately pour in the marsala (or sherry) to deglaze the pan: it will simmer and lose its raw alcohol flavour. Let it simmer for about 2 minutes, then reduce the heat to medium-low and return the chicken pieces to the pan (along with any the juices from the bowl). Simmer for 8–10 minutes – there should be very little moisture in the pan – then remove the pan from the heat and stir in the crème fraîche to warm through. Season with salt and pepper.

While the sauce simmers, cook the pasta according to the packet instructions (usually in a saucepan of salted boiling water for 8–12 minutes). Drain and toss with a small drizzle of olive oil to prevent sticking. Season with salt and pepper.

Divide the spaghetti or tagliatelle among four warm bowls. Top with the creamy chicken and mushrooms and sprinkle with the grated Parmesan and the extra thyme leaves and parsley.

Tip

Prefer a different carbohydrate base? Serve the chicken and mushroom sauce over egg noodles, cauliflower 'rice' (if you are living low carb), or any 'free-from' pasta (if you steer clear of gluten).

Harrisa Chicken and Pepper Pasta

SERVES

4

PREP: 10 mins
COOK: 20 mins, *not including the slow-cooked chicken*

300g high-protein pasta (any shape)
1 tbsp olive oil, plus extra for drizzling
½ onion, finely chopped
2 garlic cloves, crushed
100g frozen petits pois
100g chargrilled roasted red peppers (from a jar), drained and finely chopped
90g shop-bought harissa paste
100g crème fraîche
400g shredded slow-cooked chicken (see page 184) or succulent cooked and sliced chicken breasts
salt and freshly ground black pepper
handful of parsley leaves, chopped, to serve

Harissa is without doubt one of the best shop-bought pastes available. Just a tablespoon of the stuff brings so much heat and flavour to anything. I love it on chicken, fish, meatballs and pasta. This is another one of those meal-prep winners that tastes delicious cold the next day, so don't be worried about leftovers going to waste.

Cook the pasta according to the packet instructions (usually in a saucepan of salted boiling water for 8–12 minutes, depending on the shape and type). Drain – reserving about 100ml of the pasta cooking water – and drizzle with a little olive oil, tossing well to combine and prevent sticking.

Meanwhile, heat the 1 tablespoon of oil in a large frying pan over a medium heat, add the onion and cook for 6–7 minutes until softened and starting to caramelise. Stir in the garlic and cook for another minute until fragrant, then add the reserved pasta water to the pan, along with the petits pois. Cook for 2–3 minutes, then add the roasted peppers and harissa paste. Simmer for 1–2 minutes, then turn the heat down to low, stir through the crème fraîche and tip in all the shredded, cooked chicken, mixing well to evenly combine and warm the chicken through. Remove the pan from the heat and season with salt and pepper.

Serve the creamy harissa chicken over the pasta and finish with a scattering of parsley, or mix it all together before serving if you like.

Lemon Oregano Chicken and Orzo

SERVES

4

PREP: 15 mins
COOK: 40 mins

8 bone-in, skin-on chicken thighs (about 960g total)
2 red onions, cut through the root into intact wedges
1 tbsp olive oil, plus extra for drizzling
300g dried orzo
3 garlic cloves, crushed
60g ready-to-eat (cured) chorizo, cut into small dice
1 tsp dried oregano
finely grated zest of 3 lemons (preferably unwaxed)
250g cherry tomatoes, halved
50g pitted black olives, sliced
salt and freshly ground black pepper
1–2 fresh oregano sprigs, leaves picked, to serve

I love a one-pan, oven-dish dinner. Here, I use skin-on chicken thighs, which go nice and crispy, and the orzo pasta soaks up all the wonderful lemony, herby flavours. The chorizo gives it a little extra kick of flavour, too. The whole family will be polishing this one off. Absolutely delicious.

Preheat the oven to 220°C (200°C fan/gas mark 7) and line a large baking tray with baking paper.

Season the chicken thighs all over with salt and pepper and place on the tray skin side up. Roast in the oven for 20 minutes.

Meanwhile, put the red onion wedges into a bowl and drizzle over a little olive oil. Season with salt and pepper.

Once the chicken has had 20 minutes in the oven, remove the tray and turn the oven temperature down to 200°C (180°C fan/gas mark 6). Nestle the onion wedges around the chicken, brushing the rendered chicken juices over the wedges. Return the tray to the oven for another 17–19 minutes, until the chicken has cooked through.

Meanwhile, cook the orzo according to the packet instructions (usually in a saucepan of salted boiling water for 6–7 minutes). Drain well.

Heat the 1 tablespoon of olive oil in a large frying pan over a medium heat, add the garlic and chorizo and cook, stirring, for 1–2 minutes. Stir in the oregano and two-thirds of the lemon zest, then tip in the drained orzo, tomatoes and olives. Cut 2 of the zested lemons in half and squeeze in the juice, mixing well to warm through and combine. Season with salt and pepper and keep warm until the chicken is done.

Put the orzo mix on a large platter, drizzle over the chicken-tray roasting juices (for maximum flavour), then top with the chicken and roasted red onion wedges. Finish with the remaining lemon zest and the essential scattering of fresh oregano. Cut the third zested lemon into wedges to serve alongside (to boost the zing).

Tip

To air-fry the seasoned chicken, cook in a large air fryer at 180°C for 25–28 minutes, adding the oiled red onion wedges for the last 8–10 minutes.

Smoky Chicken Pasta Bake

SERVES

4

PREP: 15 mins
COOK: 30 mins

2–3 tbsp olive oil

130g Tenderstem® broccoli (long-stem/broccolini), cut into thirds

130g frozen sweetcorn kernels

3 spring onions, trimmed and thinly sliced

2 garlic cloves, crushed

8 skinless, boneless chicken thighs, cut into bite-sized pieces (about 800g)

300g any short pasta shape (preferably high-protein)

salt and freshly ground black pepper

For the sauce

30g butter

30g plain flour

1½ tsp smoked paprika, plus extra to serve

500ml full-fat milk

50g finely grated Parmesan cheese

You can't go wrong with a pasta bake. I love how everything gets thrown in the tray in 15 minutes, and then the oven does the rest. The smoked paprika and Parmesan cheese are the perfect combo. I can pretty much guarantee there'll be no leftovers with this one.

Preheat the oven to 220°C (200°C fan/gas mark 7) and have a deep baking/roasting dish ready (like a lasagne dish).

Start with the veg. Heat a drizzle of the oil in a large frying pan over a medium-high heat, add the broccoli, corn and spring onions and cook for 2–3 minutes, stirring, until the vegetables are starting to caramelise and soften but still retain their crunch. Add the garlic and cook for another minute, then transfer the vegetables to a large bowl and set aside.

Heat a little more oil in the same pan over a high heat, add half the chicken and cook for 4–5 minutes until golden brown on all sides (it doesn't need to be cooked through at this point). Remove from the pan and add to the bowl of veg and brown the remaining chicken with another drizzle of oil (this will avoid overcrowding the pan). Season with salt and pepper.

Meanwhile, cook the pasta according to the packet instructions (usually in a saucepan of salted boiling water for 8–12 minutes, depending on the shape and type). Drain and add to the bowl of vegetables and chicken. Mix, then tip out into the baking dish.

At the same time, make the sauce. Melt the butter in a saucepan over a medium heat. Add the flour and stir for about 2 minutes until the stiff mixture turns slightly darker and pulls away from the sides of the pan. Add the paprika, then drizzle in the milk, a little at a time, whisking continuously, until all the milk is added and the sauce is lump-free and starting to thicken (about 5 minutes). Stir in most of the Parmesan and season.

Pour the sauce over the pasta, scatter over the remaining Parmesan and bake in the oven for 15–16 minutes until golden. Remove from the oven and serve with another small pinch of smoked paprika on top, if you like.

Tip

Got some leftover cooked meat in the fridge? Chuck it in instead of the chicken – just add it to the pan with the veg at the end to warm through before mixing with the pasta.

Speedy Bolognese with Herby Spaghetti

SERVES

4

PREP: 10 mins
COOK: 15 mins

1 tbsp olive oil

600g 5%-fat minced beef

3 garlic cloves, crushed

3–4 thyme sprigs, leaves picked and finely chopped, plus extra to serve

2 rosemary sprigs, needles picked and finely chopped

200g passata

2 tsp honey

300g high-protein spaghetti

20g unsalted butter

drizzle of olive oil (or some more butter), to fry the eggs

4 eggs

4 generous spoonfuls of kimchi, to serve (optional)

salt and freshly ground black pepper

A slow-cooked bolognese is good, but we don't always have time to spend hours at the hob. This one takes all the same flavours and ideas but speeds things up. The rosemary and thyme really take things up to a new level, too. You might think I'm mad sticking a fried egg on top, but trust me, it works (and it gives the dish a proper protein boost). I think you will love this one and make it time and time again.

Heat the oil in a large frying pan over a high heat, add the mince and cook until the mince is browned and starting to crisp, breaking up the mince with a wooden spoon as it cooks – this can take up to 10 minutes. Add half of the garlic and half of the chopped thyme and rosemary in the last 2 minutes. Stir in the passata and honey, season with salt and pepper and cook for 1–2 minutes, stirring well, then cover and keep warm.

Meanwhile, cook the spaghetti according to the packet instructions (usually in a saucepan of salted boiling water for 8–12 minutes). Transfer to a colander to quickly drain, reserving 100ml of the pasta cooking water.

Immediately return the saucepan to the hob over a low heat. Add the butter, remaining garlic and herbs and the reserved pasta cooking water, and whisk well to emulsify, then tip the drained spaghetti back in, tossing well to evenly coat. Season with salt and pepper.

At the same time, heat some oil (or butter) in a frying pan over a medium-high heat, crack the eggs into the pan and fry until done to your liking.

Serve the spaghetti with the mince and top with a fried egg. Season with salt and pepper. If you have any thyme leaves to spare, scatter them over to fancy this simple dish up a bit! Enjoy with some kimchi alongside, if you like.

Creamy Curry Meatball Pasta

SERVES

4

PREP: 15 mins
COOK: 20 mins

700g shop-bought beef
   meatballs
olive oil, for drizzling
300g high-protein pasta (any
   shape)
salt and freshly ground
   black pepper
generous handful of parsley
   leaves, chopped, to serve

For the sauce

1 tbsp olive oil
1 onion, finely chopped
1 tbsp curry powder
¼ tsp turmeric
250ml beef stock (made with
   ½ stock cube)
2 tsp chutney or sweet chilli
   sauce
120g reduced-fat crème fraîche

Another one that always goes down a storm with all my kids. The curry sauce is rich and creamy but not too spicy – you can increase or reduce the amount of curry powder depending on your taste. I use shop-bought meatballs for speed and convenience, but you can make your own really easily with some beef mince, breadcrumbs, an egg and some salt and pepper. Just work it all together in your hands and form into small balls, then bake as described below.

Preheat the oven to 220°C (200°C fan/gas mark 7) and line a large baking tray with baking paper.

Spread the meatballs out on the tray, drizzle over a little olive oil, season with salt and pepper and bake in the oven for 15–18 minutes until cooked through, then remove.

Meanwhile, cook the pasta according to the packet instructions (usually in a saucepan of salted boiling water for 8–12 minutes, depending on the shape and type). Drain and drizzle with a little olive oil, tossing well to combine and prevent sticking.

While the meatballs are in the oven and the pasta's cooking, make the sauce. Heat the oil in a large frying pan over a medium heat, add the onion and cook for 3–4 minutes until soft and translucent. Stir in the curry powder and turmeric, then pour in the beef stock and turn the heat down to low. Simmer for 5–10 minutes or until the stock reduces by more than half, then remove the pan from the heat and stir in the chutney (or sweet chilli sauce) and the crème fraîche. Stir to combine and warm through gently. Add the baked meatballs to the sauce, tossing to coat.

Serve the saucy meatballs over the pasta, scattering parsley over just before serving.

Tip

To air-fry the oiled meatballs, cook in the air fryer in batches at 220°C for 12–14 minutes per batch, shaking the basket halfway through cooking.

VEG &
PLANT-
POWERED

Chickpea Cakes with Coriander and Lime Dip

SERVES

4

PREP: 15 mins
COOK: 25 mins, *plus cooling*

For the sesame chickpea cakes

2 x 400g tins chickpeas, drained and rinsed
6 spring onions, trimmed and roughly chopped
6 garlic cloves, roughly chopped
1 green chilli, roughly chopped (deseeded if preferred)
20g coriander, roughly chopped
20g parsley, roughly chopped
small handful of dill fronds, roughly chopped
1 tbsp ground cumin
1 tsp salt
1 egg
olive oil, for brushing and drizzling
60g white sesame seeds
salt and freshly ground black pepper
salad greens, to serve (optional)

For the coriander and lime dip

juice of 3 limes (around 1½ tbsp)
50ml olive oil
generous handful of coriander leaves, finely chopped
2 garlic cloves, crushed
pinch of chilli powder

This is my favourite way of using chickpeas in a recipe. The cakes really taste so awesome fresh out the oven with the crunchy sesame seed coating. The fresh coriander and lime dip is the ideal partner, too. These make a great snack or a starter for a dinner party.

Blitz the chickpeas in a food processor until they are roughly broken up. Add the spring onions, garlic, chilli, coriander, parsley, dill, cumin, salt and egg and continue to blend until the mixture is smooth and bright green. Do not be tempted to add liquid to the mix to help it come together, just stop the machine and scrape down the sides of the bowl. Season generously with pepper. Place the mixture in the fridge for 30 minutes to firm up (or longer – you could even make this mixture the day before).

When ready to cook, preheat the oven to 200°C (180°C fan/gas mark 6) and line a large baking tray with baking paper. Brush a little olive oil on the tray.

Form 20 balls from the mixture (33–35g each). Weigh your first one, so you can gauge the size of the remaining ones. Lightly brush each ball with olive oil.

Place the sesame seeds in a large, wide bowl and coat each little ball completely with sesame seeds, gently pressing them in. Spread the balls out on the oiled, lined tray and bake for 10 minutes, then increase the oven temperature to 220°C (200°C fan/gas mark 7) and bake for another 10–12 minutes until golden. Leave to cool for 10–15 minutes as these are best enjoyed at room temperature. They will also set a little firmer once slightly cooled.

While they cool, whisk the dip ingredients together in a small bowl. Season with salt and pepper, if needed. Serve the sesame cakes with the sauce for dipping, and enjoy with a simple salad on the side, if you like.

PROTEIN *BOOST*

Serve with Spicy Chickpea and Avocado Salad (page 148).

Tip

You can air-fry the coated balls in the lightly oiled basket (in batches) at 200°C for 15 minutes, then at 220°C for another 3–4 minutes until golden.

Lentil, Chickpea and Broccoli with Halloumi

SERVES

4

PREP: 10 mins
COOK: 15 mins

300g Tenderstem® broccoli
(long-stem/broccolini)
drizzle of olive oil
salt and freshly ground
black pepper

For the halloumi

2–3 tbsp olive oil
450g halloumi cheese, cut into
1cm-thick slices and patted
dry
finely grated zest of 1 lemon
(preferably unwaxed)

For the legume mix

1 tbsp olive oil
1 red onion, finely chopped
2 garlic cloves, crushed
235g ready-cooked lentils
(drained weight if using
tinned)
1 x 400g tin chickpeas, drained
and rinsed
100g chargrilled red peppers
(from a jar), drained and
chopped
1 lemon, cut in wedges, to serve

For the dressing

1 tbsp red wine vinegar
3 tbsp olive oil

This brilliant veggie option is ready in no time. I love roasting my broccoli in the oven with olive oil, salt and pepper. It gives it a nice char and crunch. The halloumi tastes even better with a little tang of lemon zest. This is ideal any day of the week for the ultimate healthy veggie lunch on the go.

Preheat the oven to 200°C (180°C fan/gas mark 6) and line a large baking tray with baking paper.

Toss the broccoli with the olive oil and season with salt and pepper. Spread it out evenly on the lined tray and roast in the oven for 10–12 minutes, until tender. Remove and set aside.

While the broccoli is in the oven, fry the halloumi. Heat a drizzle of the olive oil in a large, non-stick frying pan over a medium-high heat. Add half of the halloumi slices – frying is best done in batches, so they've got space to crisp up nicely – and cook for about 4 minutes (2 minutes on each side), until golden all over. Repeat with the remaining halloumi slices. Season with pepper and sprinkle with the lemon zest. Set aside.

For the legume mix, heat the oil in the same pan over a medium heat. Add the onion and garlic and cook for 1–2 minutes, stirring regularly until soft and caramelised. Squeeze in the juice of your zested lemon to deglaze the pan, then tip in the lentils, chickpeas and red peppers, stirring well to combine and gently warm through. Remove from the heat and cover to keep warm.

Make the dressing by whisking together the vinegar and oil in a small bowl.

Serve the legume mix with the roasted broccoli. Drizzle the dressing over and top with the lemony halloumi. Serve with lemon wedges alongside for an extra squeeze of zing.

Cheeky Quinoa with Mushroom and Tofu

SERVES

4

swap the soy sauce for tamari

Sesame, ginger, garlic and chilli really pack this dish with all my favourite flavours. If you've found quinoa to be quite plain in the past, I'm sure this will change your mind. Don't forget to give it a good squeeze of fresh lime juice at the end. It makes a real difference to the flavour and vibe.

PREP: 15 mins
COOK: 20 mins

200g quinoa, rinsed

3 tbsp olive oil or coconut oil

450g chestnut mushrooms, thickly sliced

2 garlic cloves, crushed

25g fresh ginger, finely grated

6 spring onions, trimmed and thinly sliced

2 tbsp soy sauce

juice of 1 lime (about 2 tsp), plus lime wedges to serve

1 red chilli, finely chopped (deseeded if preferred)

1 tbsp toasted sesame oil

salt and freshly ground black pepper

For the tofu

250g firm tofu, drained well and cut into 1.5–2cm dice

2 tsp soy sauce

1 tbsp cornflour

1 tbsp olive oil

Bring 400ml water to the boil in a saucepan. Add the quinoa, reduce the heat to medium, cover partially and simmer for 12–15 minutes until the water is absorbed and the pan is dry. Check on it regularly: the quinoa is cooked when the grains are translucent and the outer germ separates. Remove from the heat, fluff with a fork and set aside to keep warm. Season with pepper.

Meanwhile, heat the oil in a large frying pan or wok over a high heat. Add the mushrooms and stir-fry for 3–4 minutes until golden and caramelised. You might need to do this in batches, transferring each batch of caramelised mushrooms to a bowl (and adding a little more oil, if necessary). Add the garlic and ginger in the final minute of cooking your last batch of mushrooms, mixing well to cook and combine.

Reduce the heat to low, return all the mushrooms to the pan (along with any juices from the bowl), then stir in the spring onions, soy sauce, lime juice and chilli and cook for another minute until fragrant.

Remove from the heat and stir into the cooked quinoa. Drizzle with the sesame oil and toss well to combine. Set aside.

Toss the diced tofu in a bowl with the soy sauce and cornflour. Heat the oil in a frying pan over a high heat, add the tofu, and fry until golden on all sides. Drain on a plate lined with kitchen paper, then gently toss with the quinoa and mushroom mix.

Divide among four warm bowls, with lime wedges served alongside to squeeze over, if you like.

PROTEIN
BOOST

Add 200g crispy
seasoned tempeh,
(see page 128).

Spicy Mixed Bean Chilli Bowl

SERVES

4

swap the
soy sauce
for tamari

PREP: 15 mins
COOK: 15 mins

280g uncooked basmati rice
4 eggs
2 ripe avocados, stoned, peeled
    and thinly sliced
80g feta cheese, crumbled
pinch of dried chilli flakes
handful of coriander, chopped
salt and freshly ground
    black pepper
1 lime, cut into wedges, to serve

For the mixed bean chilli

1 tbsp olive oil
1 onion, finely chopped
1 red pepper, diced
2 garlic cloves, crushed
2 tsp ground cumin
1 tsp smoked paprika
1 tsp ground coriander
½ tsp chilli powder
1 tsp dried oregano
1 tbsp double-concentrated
    tomato puree
1 x 400g tin chopped tomatoes
1 x 400g tin black beans,
    drained and rinsed
1 x 400g tin kidney beans,
    drained and rinsed
1 tbsp soy sauce

This fully loaded chilli bowl is an ideal meal: it's got the perfect balance of protein, fat, carbohydrate and fibre. It's a great one for batch cooking too, so doubling up the ingredients of the chilli is a good idea. I often serve the chilli the following day on rice or jacket potatoes. Expect windy conditions from all the beans. Better out than in, LOL.

First, make the mixed bean chilli. Heat the oil in a large frying pan or wok over a medium heat. Add the onion and red pepper and cook for 5–6 minutes until softened, then stir in the garlic and cook for another minute until fragrant. Add the cumin, smoked paprika, coriander, chilli powder, oregano and tomato puree and cook for 30 seconds before adding the tomatoes, then fill the empty tin of tomatoes about a third full with water, swirl it in the tin, then tip the water into the pan. Add the black beans, kidney beans and soy sauce, then lower the heat to medium and simmer for 5–7 minutes, until the mixture is thick and chunky. Taste and adjust the seasoning with salt and pepper. Remove from the heat and keep warm.

While the chilli cooks, cook the rice according to the packet instructions (usually in a saucepan of boiling water for 10–15 minutes). Once cooked, drain the rice in a sieve and season with salt.

Fry the eggs in oil to your liking.

Divide the warm rice among four bowls and serve with the spicy bean mix. Top each portion with a fried egg, the avocado and the feta. Finish with the chilli flakes and coriander. Serve with lime wedges to squeeze over the whole lot.

PROTEIN *BOOST*

Add a boiled egg or try roasted chickpeas (see page 148) as a crunchy topping.

Crispy Tempeh, Miso and Roasted Veg

SERVES

4

or more as a side dish

swap the soy sauce for tamari

PREP: 15 mins
COOK: 20 mins

1 red pepper, deseeded and
    roughly chopped
1 courgette, roughly chopped
2 tbsp olive oil
200g uncooked wild rice or
    white rice (or a mix of both)
salt and freshly ground
    black pepper
handful of parsley leaves,
    chopped, to serve

For the tempeh

400g tempeh, cut into
    2–3cm dice
1½ tbsp soy sauce
1 tbsp olive oil
1 tsp garlic powder
½ tsp smoked paprika

For the lemon miso dressing

40g white miso paste
juice of 1½ lemons (about
    3 tbsp)
1 tbsp olive oil
1 tsp maple syrup (or honey for
    non-vegan option)
1 garlic clove, crushed

Nothing beats roasted veg. For me, they taste so much better than when they are boiled or steamed. They take on a whole new life. My kids love it when I throw loads of veg in the oven with some olive oil and spices and serve them up all caramelised and crispy. The lemon miso dressing drizzled over the rice that is served with the crispy tempeh and veg is an outstanding finishing touch. A top dish.

Preheat the oven to 200°C (180°C fan/gas mark 6) and line two baking trays (one of them should be large) with baking paper.

Toss the chopped pepper and courgette with the olive oil. Season with salt and pepper and spread out on the large lined baking tray.

Toss the diced tempeh with the soy sauce, olive oil, garlic powder and smoked paprika together in a bowl, then spread it out on the second lined tray.

Place the trays in the oven and cook for 20 minutes until the vegetables are roasted and tender and the tempeh is crispy and golden.

While the vegetables and tempeh are in the oven, cook the rice according to the packet instructions (usually in a saucepan of boiling water for 10–15 minutes: wild rice may take 3–4 minutes longer). Once cooked, drain the rice in a sieve and season with salt.

Make the dressing by whisking together all the ingredients in a small bowl.

Combine the cooked rice and roasted veg. Top with the crispy tempeh and drizzle over the lemon miso dressing. Finish with a scattering of chopped parsley to serve.

Tip

To air-fry the seasoned tempeh, cook in the air fryer at 200°C for 10–12 minutes, shaking the basket halfway through.

Sweet Potato, Lentil and Goat's Cheese

SERVES

4

or more as
a side dish

PREP: 15 mins
COOK: 25+ mins

40g mixed seeds
1 tbsp olive oil
1 onion, finely chopped
3 garlic cloves, crushed
3 x 400g tins ready-cooked
  lentils, drained
1½ tsp ground cumin
1½ tsp ground paprika
200g baby spinach
240g goat's cheese
2 tbsp honey

For the sweet potato wedges

3 medium sweet potatoes
  (about 670g), scrubbed clean
  and cut into 3–4cm-thick
  wedges (skin on)
1 tsp ground cumin
1 tsp ground paprika
1 tbsp olive oil
salt and freshly ground
  black pepper

This is one of the most satisfying veggie recipes – a real sweet treat. The goat's cheese paired with the sweet, caramelised potatoes and a cheeky drizzle of honey is just the best. If you prefer a different cheese, try ricotta, feta or mozzarella: they all work well. Eating lentils is a great way to get some extra gut-healthy plant power in your tummy.

First, cook the sweet potatoes. Preheat the oven to 230°C (210°C fan/gas mark 8) and line a large baking tray with baking paper.

Spread the sweet potato wedges out on the lined baking tray, sprinkle with the spices, and season with salt and pepper. Drizzle with olive oil and brush the seasoning evenly over all the wedges. Roast in the oven for 25 minutes until golden and caramelised: slide a sharp knife into them, they should be tender. Thicker wedges may need 2–3 minutes longer, so remove the ones that are done to ensure they do not burn. Set aside and keep warm.

Meanwhile, prepare all the other tasty bits. Toast the mixed seeds in a large, dry frying pan or wok over a medium-high heat for 3–4 minutes until they pop and become fragrant. Tip them out of the pan and set aside.

Add the oil to the same pan and set the heat to medium. Add the onion and cook for 3–4 minutes until soft and translucent, then cook for another 2–3 minutes, stirring, until it starts to turn golden and caramelise. Add the garlic and cook for another minute until fragrant. Tip in the drained lentils, cumin and paprika, stir well to combine and reduce the heat to medium-low. Tip in the spinach, stirring continuously until wilted. The mixture is ready when there is no moisture in the pan. Season to taste, if needed. Stir in most of the toasted mixed seeds.

Divide the lentil and spinach mix among four warm plates or bowls and top with the wedges. Crumble over the cheese and drizzle with the honey. Scatter over the remaining seeds and serve.

Tip

To air-fry the sweet potato wedges, cook at 200°C for 20 minutes, shaking the basket halfway through.

PROTEIN BOOST

Serve with a plant-based, non-ultra-processed meat substitute, such as tempeh.

Roasted Butternut Squash and Lentil Stew

SERVES

4

PREP: 15 mins
COOK: 25 mins

500g peeled butternut squash, cut into 3cm pieces
1 tbsp olive oil
½ tsp garam masala
½ tsp garlic powder
30g pumpkin seeds
20g desiccated coconut
salt and freshly ground black pepper
4 tbsp coconut yoghurt, to serve

For the fragrant lentil stew

70g creamed coconut block, roughly chopped
1 tbsp olive oil
1 onion, finely chopped
1 medium carrot, peeled and finely chopped
1 celery stalk, finely chopped
2 garlic cloves, crushed
1 tsp garam masala
½ tsp ground cumin
¼ tsp ground turmeric
1 x 400g tin ready-cooked lentils, drained
1 x 400g tin white beans (borlotti or cannellini), drained and rinsed
3 tbsp double-concentrated tomato puree
150g baby spinach

Here's a really heart-warming and gut-healthy stew. Butternut squash is one of those veggies that takes a bit of love and effort to make into a meal, but it's always worth it. When it's roasted, it becomes deliciously sticky and sweet. This stew has lentils and white beans too, so there's plenty of plant protein and goodness for your tummy.

Preheat the oven to 210°C (190°C fan/gas mark 6) and line a baking tray with baking paper.

Toss the squash with the olive oil, garam masala and garlic powder, season with salt and pepper and spread the chunks out on the lined baking tray. Roast in the oven for 17–20 minutes until golden and tender.

Meanwhile, toast the pumpkin seeds in a large, dry frying pan or wok over a medium-high heat for 4–5 minutes until they pop and become crispy. Tip into a bowl and set aside. Add the desiccated coconut to the same dry pan and toast for 2–3 minutes until golden, stirring regularly (it can burn quickly), then add it to the bowl of pumpkin seeds – these are your tasty garnishes.

Add 280ml boiling-hot water to a heatproof jug and add the creamed coconut pieces. Leave to dissolve, whisking if necessary.

Heat the olive oil in the same pan you used to toast the seeds and coconut, over a medium heat. Add the onion, carrot and celery and cook for 4–5 minutes until softened, then stir in the garlic and cook for another minute until fragrant. Add the spices, stir well to coat the vegetables, then tip in the lentils, beans, tomato puree and the coconut milk. Tip in the spinach (several handfuls at a time), allowing it to wilt into the mixture. Simmer for 8–10 minutes, until thickened. Season to taste.

To serve, divide the lentil mixture among four warm bowls and top with the roasted butternut chunks. Add a dollop of coconut yoghurt to each portion, then finish with a scattering of the toasted pumpkin seed and coconut garnish.

VEG & PLANT-POWERED

Daddy's Top Veggie Bolognese

SERVES

4

PREP: 10 mins
COOK: 25 mins

1 tbsp olive oil, plus extra for drizzling
1 onion, finely chopped
1 carrot, peeled and finely chopped
1 celery stalk, finely chopped
300g chestnut mushrooms, finely chopped
2 garlic cloves, crushed
1 tsp dried oregano
½ tsp smoked paprika
½ tsp dried chilli flakes (optional)
1 tbsp double-concentrated tomato puree
1 x 400g tin chopped tomatoes
1 x 400g tin ready-cooked lentils, drained
1 tbsp soy sauce
2 tsp honey
300g high-protein spaghetti
generous handful of basil leaves
salt and freshly ground black pepper
4 tsp finely grated Parmesan cheese (optional), to serve

I made this for my kids one night without telling them it had no mince in. I wanted to see if they noticed. Great news! They didn't, and they ate the lot. I use most of the same ingredients and flavours you expect in a meat bolognese, but the veggies and lentils do the job of replacing the meat. You won't miss the beef and will be fully satisfied. Give it a try. A little more veg protein in our body can only be a positive thing.

Heat the 1 tablespoon of olive oil in a large frying pan or wok over a medium heat. Add the onion, carrot and celery and cook for 8–10 minutes until soft and translucent, then stir in the mushrooms, garlic, oregano, smoked paprika and chilli flakes (if using) and cook for a further 2 minutes until fragrant.

Add the tomato puree and chopped tomatoes, then fill the empty tomato tin about half full with water, swirl it in the tin and tip the water into the pan, along with the lentils. Stir well to combine and simmer for about 10 minutes or until the mixture is chunky and free of excess liquid. Stir in the soy sauce and honey, then season with salt and pepper.

Meanwhile, cook the spaghetti according to the packet instructions (usually in a saucepan of salted boiling water for 8–12 minutes). Drain and toss with a drizzle of olive oil to prevent sticking, and season with a little salt.

Just before serving, thinly slice most of the basil and stir it through the chunky lentil mixture to combine.

Divide the spaghetti among four warm bowls and top with the chunky lentil mix, or mix them together. Sprinkle with the grated Parmesan (if using). Season generously with more black pepper and scatter over the remaining basil leaves just before serving.

Ohhhhh Bergine and Lentil Bake

SERVES

4

**PREP: 15 mins
COOK: 40 mins**

2 aubergines, trimmed and
   thinly sliced (about 5mm thick)
generous drizzle of olive oil
salt and freshly ground
   black pepper

For the filling

2 tbsp olive oil
1 onion, finely chopped
1 carrot, peeled and grated
3 garlic cloves, crushed
250g chestnut mushrooms,
   finely chopped
2 tsp dried oregano
2 tsp ground cinnamon
1 tsp smoked paprika
1 x 400g tin chopped tomatoes
2 x 400g tins ready-cooked
   lentils, drained
2 tbsp tamari

For the top layer

4 eggs
85g cream cheese
2 tbsp double cream
pinch of ground nutmeg
pinch of ground cinnamon

This is inspired by a classic moussaka but it's quicker to make and even tastier. It has all the sexy flavours going on – oregano, cinnamon, paprika – and uses a simple cream cheese topping, which tastes and smells unreal when it wafts out of the oven. Serve it with a fresh salad and a splash of hot sauce and you are good to go.

Preheat the oven to 220°C (200°C fan/gas mark 7) and line your largest baking tray with baking paper.

Lay out the slices of aubergine on the lined tray, overlapping them if needed, to fit. Drizzle with the olive oil, season with salt and pepper and bake in the oven for 10 minutes. This precooks the aubergine. Set the aubergine aside, but do not turn off the oven.

While the aubergine is in the oven, start the filling. Heat the oil in a large frying pan or wok over a medium-high heat, add the onion and carrot and cook for 7–8 minutes until they start to caramelise. Stir in the garlic, mushrooms, oregano, cinnamon and paprika and cook for another 2–3 minutes until fragrant. Add the chopped tomatoes, stir well and simmer for 5–7 minutes, then tip in the lentils and tamari and stir to warm through for 2–3 minutes. The mixture should be free of excess moisture, so increase the heat and stir continuously until it reaches this point. Season with salt and pepper.

To assemble the bake, arrange half the precooked aubergine slices in the bottom of a deep baking/roasting dish (like a lasagne dish). Spoon over the lentil mixture, then top with a layer of the remaining aubergine slices. Make the top layer by whisking the eggs, cream cheese and cream together until smooth. Season with salt and pepper, and add the nutmeg and cinnamon. Pour it over the dish and bake in the oven for 20 minutes, until golden and the egg layer has cooked through.

PROTEIN *BOOST*

Serve with a black bean salad or chickpea salad, like the ones on pages 145 and 148.

Fancy-pants Omelette

SERVES

4

PREP: 5 mins
COOK: 10 mins

8 eggs, whisked
olive oil (or butter), for frying
4 large serving spoons of
    4-Herb 'Ratatouille' (see
    page 69)
80g feta cheese, crumbled
salt and freshly ground
    black pepper

I love to start the day with eggs, but, let's be honest, scrambled eggs and plain omelettes on repeat get real boring real quick. This omelette uses some of that lovely ratatouille-style veg from page 69. Add some crumbled feta cheese and you've got yourself a very tasty, fancy-pants omelette.

Make the omelette mix by whisking the eggs in a bowl. Season with salt and pepper.

Heat a drizzle of olive oil (or a piece of butter) in a large, non-stick frying pan over a medium-low heat.

Making one omelette at a time, pour a quarter of the whisked egg mix into the pan and cook, undisturbed, for 2–3 minutes until the edges start to set. Add a quarter of the cooked veggies evenly over one side of the omelette, then sprinkle over a quarter of the crumbled feta. Carefully fold the omelette in half and let it cook for another minute. Slide onto a plate and keep warm.

Repeat the process, adding more oil (or butter) for each omlette, using all the remaining ingredients until 4 omelettes are made. Eat straight away.

PROTEIN
BOOST

Use 3 eggs per
omelette and cook it
a little longer.

I Prefer a Quiche

SERVES

4

PREP: 15 mins
COOK: 30–35 mins

2 tbsp olive oil
100g baby spinach
2 garlic cloves, crushed
20g pitted Kalamata olives,
    sliced
10g baby capers, drained
    (about 1 tbsp)
140g cherry tomatoes, halved
8 eggs
80g crème fraîche
80g cream cheese
1 tsp dried herbes de Provence
50g feta cheese, crumbled
salt and freshly ground
    black pepper
handful of basil leaves, to serve
green salad or steamed green
    vegetables, to serve
    (optional)

Oooh, look at me I'm crustless, which means I'm simple to make. I haven't got the time or the patience to make a proper quiche with a fancy made-from-scratch pastry crust, but this tastes just as good. It has all the greatest flavours of the Mediterranean, including juicy tomatoes, creamy feta and salty olives. Serve it with a simple side salad for the win.

Preheat the oven to 200°C (180°C fan/gas mark 6). Grease a large, round baking tin (about 20cm in diameter, and at least 3cm deep) and line it with baking paper.

Heat the oil in a large frying pan or wok over a medium-high heat. Add the spinach and cook for 2–3 minutes until the spinach has completely wilted and the pan is dry – this is important, to prevent a soggy quiche. Add the garlic and cook for a further 1–2 minutes, stirring continuously to prevent the garlic burning. Remove the pan from the heat and mix in the olives, capers and tomatoes.

Whisk the eggs, crème fraîche and cream cheese in a large bowl until completely smooth. Stir in the herbes de Provence, and season with salt and very generously with pepper.

Pour the egg mixture into the prepared tin, then tip in the spinach mix, ensuring it's evenly combined. Scatter over the crumbled feta cheese, then bake in the oven for 18–20 minutes until the centre is cooked through.

After 20 minutes, turn off the oven and leave the quiche to cook gently for another 5–10 minutes in the residual heat. Remove from the oven and leave to cool before slicing into four to eight wedges.

To serve, tear or slice the basil and scatter it evenly over each portion. Enjoy as is, or with a lovely fresh salad or steamed greens on the side.

PROTEIN *BOOST*

Scatter over toasted pine nuts to serve, for crunch.

LUNCHBOX
INSPO

Soba Noodle Edamame Salad

SERVES

2

or 4 as a side salad

PREP: 15 mins
COOK: 10 mins

50g cashew nuts
100g soba noodles (2 nests)
drizzle of olive oil (optional)
200g shelled edamame beans (defrosted if frozen)
1 small carrot, peeled and grated
½ red pepper, deseeded and thinly sliced
2 spring onions, trimmed and thinly sliced on the diagonal
1 tbsp sesame seeds
handful of coriander leaves, chopped

For the sesame ginger dressing

2 tbsp toasted sesame oil
1 tbsp low-sodium soy sauce
1 tbsp rice wine vinegar
1 tsp maple syrup (or honey for non-vegan option)
15g fresh ginger, finely grated
1 small garlic clove, crushed
salt and freshly ground black pepper

This is the kind of lunch you eat and genuinely feel more energised after. This vibrant salad topped with crunchy roasted cashew nuts is packed with edamame beans, which are a great source of protein and can be found in the freezer aisle of most supermarkets. The zingy dressing brings it all together and is super easy to make. Go and fuel yourself right today.

Preheat the oven to 190°C (170°C fan/gas mark 5) and line a small baking tray with baking paper. Spread the cashew nuts out on the tray and toast in the oven for 6–8 minutes. Leave to cool, then roughly chop. Set aside.

Meanwhile, roughly break up the soba noodle nests and cook according to the packet instructions (usually in a saucepan of boiling water for 4–5 minutes). Drain and keep in a bowl of cold water to chill and prevent sticking, or drain well and toss in a little olive oil.

At the same time, cook the edamame in a small saucepan of boiling water for 3–4 minutes until tender. Drain and rinse under cold running water, then leave to cool.

Combine the edamame, carrot, red pepper, spring onions, sesame seeds and coriander in a large bowl. Drain the noodles well and add to the bowl, along with the edamame beans.

Whisk the dressing ingredients together. Season with salt and pepper, then pour it over the salad, tossing well to combine. Finish with a scattering of the toasted cashew nuts before serving.

Enjoy immediately or store in a sealed container in the fridge for up to 2–3 days, keeping the nuts separately and scattering over just before serving.

Black Bean and Mixed Veg Salad

SERVES

2

or 4 as a
side salad

PREP: 10 mins
COOK: 5 mins

15g mixed seeds
150g shelled edamame beans
(defrosted if frozen)
60g frozen sweetcorn kernels
1 x 400g tin black beans,
drained and rinsed
120g Savoy cabbage, shredded
or thinly sliced
90g baby plum tomatoes,
quartered
50g feta cheese, crumbled
handful of coriander leaves,
chopped

For the cumin-lime dressing

2 tbsp olive oil
juice of 1 lime (about 2 tsp)
1 tsp honey
½ tsp ground cumin
salt and freshly ground
black pepper

This fresh, colourful and vibrant plate of food is proper feel-good food. Whenever I eat it, I feel energised for hours after. It makes me realise I don't always need to be eating animal proteins at every meal. In fact, I think focussing more on eating plant-based protein is really good for our health.

Toast the mixed seeds in a large, dry frying pan over a medium-high heat for 2–3 minutes until they pop and become fragrant. Remove from the pan and set aside.

Meanwhile, cook the edamame and corn in a small pan of boiling water for 3–4 minutes until tender. Drain and rinse in a sieve under cold running water, then leave to cool.

Combine the cooled edamame and corn with the black beans, cabbage, tomatoes, feta and coriander in a large bowl.

Make the dressing by whisking together all the ingredients in a small bowl. Season with salt and pepper. Pour the dressing over the salad, toss well to coat and scatter over the toasted seeds before serving.

Enjoy immediately or store the salad in the fridge in a sealed container for up to 2–3 days, keeping the seeds separately and scattering over just before serving.

Tip

This works brilliantly as a fresh wrap filling for 3–4 soft tortillas.

PROTEIN
BOOST

Add 200g cooked and seasoned tempeh (see page 128).

Spicy Chickpea and Avocado Salad

SERVES

2

or 4 as a
side salad

PREP: 15 mins
COOK: 25 mins

1 x 400g tin chickpeas,
   drained and rinsed
1 tbsp olive oil
1 tsp salt, plus extra for
   seasoning
½ tsp smoked paprika
½ tsp ground cumin
½ tsp cayenne pepper
40g wild rocket
80g baby plum tomatoes,
   halved
2 baby cucumbers, diced or
   sliced (if you're using regular
   cucumbers, remove the
   watery core)
1 ripe avocado, stoned, peeled
   and diced or sliced
4 soft-boiled eggs, halved
freshly ground black pepper

For the coriander and lime dressing

juice of 1 lime (about 2 tsp)
1 tbsp olive oil
1 garlic clove, crushed
generous handful of coriander
   leaves, chopped

This is your chance to taste oven-roasted, crispy, crunchy chickpeas, if you haven't already. They taste a million times better than cold ones out of the tin. I coat them in paprika, cumin and cayenne pepper, so they have lots of heat and flavour, before roasting them. It's easy to rely on long shelf-life, shop-bought salad dressings, but they contain loads of ingredients you don't really want in your tummy. This lime and coriander dressing is ready in minutes and brings ultimate freshness to the salad.

When ready to cook, preheat the oven to 220°C (200°C fan/gas mark 7) and line a baking tray with baking paper.

Pat the drained chickpeas dry with kitchen paper, then put them in a bowl and add the olive oil, salt, smoked paprika, cumin and cayenne pepper. Season generously with black pepper and toss well to combine. Spread out on the lined baking tray and toast in the oven for 25 minutes until dried and crunchy. How long they take will depend on how well you initially dried them. Be careful when checking on them in the oven, as they tend to spit and pop. Once done, remove and set aside.

Meanwhile, make the dressing by whisking together all the ingredients in a small bowl and seasoning to taste.

Combine the rocket, tomatoes, baby cucumbers and avocado in a large bowl. Add the dressing and toss gently to coat. Top with the halved eggs and add the crispy chickpeas just before serving.

Enjoy immediately or store the salad in the fridge in an airtight container for up to 2–3 days, keeping in mind that the avocado may lose its freshness after the first day. Keep the dressing and crispy chickpeas separately, adding them just before serving to ensure the rocket doesn't wilt and the elements retain their crunch.

Tip

To toast the seasoned chickpeas in an air fryer, cook at 190°C for 10–12 minutes until crunchy, shaking the basket regularly so they do not burn.

Spinach, Lentil and Beetroot Salad

SERVES

2

or 4 as a
side salad

PREP: 15 mins
COOK: 10 mins

50g frozen petits pois
20g pumpkin seeds
100g whole, cooked beetroots
   (fresh vacuum-packed, not
   the tinned kind)
80g goat's cheese (or
   alternative, see Tip)
250g cooked puy lentils
   (fresh or tinned)
80g baby spinach
handful of mint leaves,
   thinly sliced
2 tbsp olive oil
2½ tsp red wine vinegar
salt and freshly ground
   black pepper

Imagine if Popeye was on a diet and trying to get in better shape: this is the sort of spinach salad he would eat. As you may have noticed, I do love a toasted nut or seed on top of my salads. I think it's so important to have that crunchy texture in the mix – it just makes a standard salad so much tastier.

Cook the petits pois in a small saucepan of boiling water for 3–4 minutes until tender. Drain and rinse under cold running water, then leave to cool.

Toast the pumpkin seeds in a dry frying pan over a medium-high heat for 4–5 minutes until they pop and become crispy. Set aside.

Thinly slice the beetroot and the goat's cheese. Add to a large bowl along with the lentils, peas, baby spinach and mint.

Whisk the olive oil and red wine vinegar together, season with salt and pepper and drizzle over the salad, tossing gently to combine. Scatter over the toasted pumpkin seeds just before serving.

Enjoy immediately or store the salad in the fridge in an airtight container for up to 2–3 days, keeping the dressing and toasted pumpkin seeds separately and adding them just before serving, to ensure the spinach doesn't wilt and the seeds retain their crunch.

Tip

If goat's cheese isn't your thing, swap in feta – the combination works brilliantly. Simple, tasty and satisfying.

Uber-quick Egg Wraps

SERVES

2

PREP: 5–10 mins
COOK: 5–10 mins

Scrambled egg and salsa wraps

PROTEIN: 26g per wrap

50g baby plum tomatoes, finely chopped
2 tsp olive oil
4 eggs, whisked
¼ small red onion, finely chopped
small handful of coriander leaves, finely chopped
pinch of dried chilli flakes (optional)
2 soft high-protein tortillas
salt and freshly ground black pepper

Boiled egg and hummus wraps

PROTEIN: 23g per wrap

4 eggs
20g white sesame seeds
1 tsp smoked paprika
small pinch of dried chilli flakes (optional)
2 tbsp mayonnaise
40g hummus
2 soft high-protein tortillas
45g baby spinach leaves
salt and freshly ground black pepper

Wraps are a total godsend on busy mornings when you are in a rush to get out of the door. For me that's most days, LOL. With four hungry kids wrapped around me, I often turn to these at breakfast or lunch. I've included two filling ideas: soft scrambled eggs and salsa, and chopped boiled eggs with a layer of hummus. Both are absolutely banging, to be honest. Wrap them in foil and you've got yourself a cracking lunch to take to work or school.

Put the finely chopped tomatoes in a sieve over a bowl (this allows the excess moisture from the tomatoes to drain away, which prevents a soggy wrap).

Heat the oil in a large frying pan over a medium heat, then reduce the heat to low, add the whisked eggs and cook – stirring – until scrambled. Remove from the heat, season with salt and pepper and set aside.

Combine the drained tomatoes with the red onion and coriander. Stir in the chilli flakes (if using) and season with salt and pepper. This is your mini salsa.

Assemble the wraps by spooning over equal amounts of the scrambled eggs on each tortilla. Top with the salsa, then fold in the sides of the tortilla and roll tightly from the bottom up. If enjoying the next day, wrap tightly in foil and keep in the fridge.

Hard-boil the eggs in a pan of boiling water for 8–10 minutes, then transfer to a bowl of cold water. Once cooled, peel and finely chop the eggs.

Meanwhile, toast the sesame seeds in a dry frying pan over a medium-high heat for 3–4 minutes until golden. Remove the pan from the heat and stir in the smoked paprika and chilli flakes (if using). Add this to the chopped eggs, along with the mayonnaise. Season with salt and pepper and mix well to combine.

Spread the hummus evenly over both tortillas, then layer with baby spinach and the egg mix. Fold in the sides of the tortilla and roll tightly from the bottom up. If enjoying the next day, wrap tightly in foil and keep in the fridge.

Grab-and-go Quinoa Salad

SERVES

2

swap the soy sauce for tamari

PREP: 10 mins
COOK: 10–15 mins, *plus cooling*

100g mixed quinoa (white, red and black), rinsed

1 tbsp olive oil

1½ tbsp soy sauce

4 eggs

100g baby plum tomatoes, halved

2 baby cucumbers, sliced or diced

salt and freshly ground black pepper

This is a perfect example of fast food made healthy. If we can get into the habit of making things like this for work and when we travel, we really can live a much healthier life. Quinoa is high in protein and when combined with the boiled eggs it makes a really filling and satisfying lunch that's way better than any sandwich meal-deal from the supermarket.

Bring 200ml water to the boil in a saucepan. Add the quinoa, reduce the heat to medium, cover partially with a lid and simmer for 9–12 minutes until all the water is absorbed and the pan is dry. Check on it regularly: the quinoa is cooked when the little grains are translucent, and the outer germ separates. Fluff the quinoa with a fork and let it cool slightly, then add the olive oil and soy sauce, season with pepper and mix to combine.

While the quinoa is cooking, boil the eggs (5–6 minutes for soft yolks; 8–10 minutes for set yolks), then transfer to a bowl of cold water. Once cool, peel off the shell and slice each one into quarters. Season with salt and pepper, if desired.

Combine the seasoned quinoa, tomatoes and cucumbers. Top with the quartered eggs before serving.

Enjoy immediately or store the salad in the fridge in an airtight container for up to 2 days (soft-boiled eggs are best enjoyed on the same day they are cooked).

PROTEIN *BOOST*

Serve with extra eggs, or toasted chickpeas (see page 148) for extra crunch.

Tip

You can batch-cook an ingredient like quinoa in advance, as it stays fresh in the fridge for up to 3-4 days.

Easy Egg and Pea Salad

SERVES

2

PREP: 5 mins
COOK: 10 mins

4 eggs
60g frozen petits pois
40g wild rocket
¼ red onion, thinly sliced
salt and freshly ground
    black pepper

For the dill and mustard dressing

70g plain (natural) yoghurt,
    preferably Greek yoghurt
½ tbsp olive oil
1 tsp Dijon mustard
generous handful of dill fronds,
    chopped

Speed is king when it comes to making a healthy diet work. This is one of those fast but super-nutritious lunch ideas. When you fuel your body with stuff like this that's full of protein, healthy fats and fibre, you will find your energy levels remain so much more stable. The dill and mustard dressing with yoghurt is absolutely yummy, too.

Hard-boil the eggs in a pan of boiling water for 8–10 minutes, then transfer to a bowl of cold water. Once cooled, peel and either thinly slice or finely chop the eggs. Season them with salt and pepper.

While the eggs are boiling, cook the petits pois in a small saucepan of boiling water for 3–4 minutes until tender. Drain, rinse under cold running water, and leave to cool.

Make the dressing by whisking together all the ingredients in a small bowl. Season with salt and plenty of pepper.

Put the dressing in a large bowl or on a large serving plate. Add the eggs, peas, rocket and red onion. Toss to evenly coat before serving.

Enjoy straight away or keep it in the fridge in an airtight container for 1–2 days, keeping the dressing separately and adding it just before serving to ensure the rocket doesn't wilt.

Tip

You can use this mix as a tasty filling for soft tortillas – it will make enough for 3–4 wraps.

PROTEIN *BOOST*

For non veggies,
serve with chicken.

Salmon, Avocado and Bulgur Wheat Salad

SERVES

2

PREP: 10 mins
COOK: 20–25 mins, *plus cooling*

60g bulgur wheat, rinsed
70g soft butterhead lettuce, roughly chopped
2 baby cucumbers, diced or sliced
½ ripe avocado, stoned, peeled and sliced
2 spring onions, trimmed and thinly sliced
2 hot-smoked salmon fillets (about 180g total), skin removed (see Tip)
2 tbsp white sesame seeds, to serve

For the sesame soy dressing

2 tbsp low-sodium soy sauce
1 tbsp toasted sesame oil
1½ tsp rice wine vinegar
½ tsp honey
1 garlic clove, crushed

This is a great salad to prep ahead and enjoy cold. If you haven't cooked bulgur wheat before, don't be put off. It's very easy. It's also so good for your gut health to consume a variety of nutrients and plants, so foods like bulgur, quinoa, lentils and chickpeas are all brilliant choices and a step in the right direction for a healthier, happier gut. You will also love the simple sesame soy dressing on this one.

Cook the bulgur wheat in a saucepan of boiling water for 10–15 minutes, until the bulgur is tender (or according to the packet instructions). Drain, fluff the bulgur with a fork and let it cool.

Combine the cooled bulgur, lettuce, cucumbers, avocado and spring onions in a large bowl. Roughly flake the salmon into the bowl.

Make the dressing by whisking together all the ingredients in a small bowl.

Drizzle the dressing over the salad, tossing gently to combine. Scatter over the sesame seeds just before enjoying.

Enjoy immediately or store the salad in the fridge in an airtight container for up to 2–3 days, keeping in mind that the avocado may lose its freshness after the first day and keeping the dressing separately, adding it just before serving to ensure the lettuce doesn't wilt. Check the date on your store-bought salmon to ensure its freshness.

Tip

Don't discard salmon skin! Scrape off any flesh, lay the skin (scale side up) in an air fryer, season and cook at 190°C for 8–12 minutes until crisp. Cool, break it up and use as a snack or crunchy garnish.

Tuna and Avocado Rice Bowl

SERVES

2

swap the
soy sauce for
tamari

PREP: 10 mins

250g packet of ready-cooked
  basmati rice
2 tsp rice wine vinegar
2 spring onions, trimmed and
  thinly sliced
1 baby cucumber, sliced or diced
200g drained tinned tuna
  (in brine)
1 ripe avocado, stoned, peeled
  and diced or sliced
salt and freshly ground
  black pepper
1 tsp white sesame seeds,
  to serve

**For the ginger sesame
dressing**

1 tbsp olive oil
1 tbsp toasted sesame oil
2 tsp soy sauce
juice of ½ lime (about 1 tsp)
10g fresh ginger, finely grated

Tinned tuna is a simple and affordable source of protein, so I wanted to come up with a recipe that makes it taste really good. This one does just that. The ginger, sesame dressing gives the fish so much flavour, and the sneaky sprinkle of sesame seeds provides that special crunchy contrast in texture we always want.

Add the cooked rice to a bowl and stir in the rice wine vinegar, spring onions, cucumber, tuna and avocado. Season with salt and pepper and toss well to combine.

Make the dressing by whisking together all the ingredients in a small bowl. Drizzle the dressing over the salad and finish with a scattering of sesame seeds.

Enjoy immediately or store the salad in the fridge in an airtight container for up to 2–3 days, keeping in mind that the avocado may lose its freshness after the first day and storing the dressing separately.

Fantastic Fishcakes with Sweet Chilli Mayo

SERVES

2   ❄

PREP: 15 mins
COOK: 30 mins, *plus cooling*

1 medium potato, peeled
(about 250g peeled weight)
and diced (no bigger than
2cm)
250g drained tinned wild-
caught salmon or tuna
3 spring onions, trimmed and
thinly sliced
finely grated zest of 1 lemon
(preferably unwaxed)
handful of coriander leaves,
finely chopped
handful of parsley leaves,
finely chopped
20g crème fraîche
salt and freshly ground
black pepper
olive oil, for drizzling
salad, to serve (optional)

For the crumb

80g plain flour
1 egg, whisked
80g shop-bought dried
breadcrumbs
30g white sesame seeds
olive oil, for shallow frying

For the sweet chilli mayo

50g mayonnaise
30g sweet chilli sauce

These little belters are, as the title suggests, fantastic. You can batch cook and freeze them, so they are a good one to double up so you have some for another time. When they come out of the pan, they are crisp and golden on the outside and soft and potatoey on the inside. The sweet chilli sauce mixed with mayo is such a top combo for your dip.

Put the diced potato in a saucepan of cold water, bring to the boil and cook for about 25 minutes until completely tender, then drain in a colander. Allow to steam dry for 2–3 minutes in the colander, then transfer to a large bowl (or back into the empty saucepan, off the heat) and mash well with a potato masher.

Add the tinned fish, spring onions, lemon zest, herbs and crème fraîche to the potato and season generously. Mix well to evenly combine, then split the mixture into 12 even-sized portions, about 45g each, and shape into miniature patties.

For the crumb, prepare three shallow bowls, one with the flour (lightly season it with salt), one with the whisked egg and one with the breadcrumbs mixed with the sesame seeds.

Lightly dust a patty with the flour, then dip it into the egg, allowing the excess egg to drip off. Gently roll in the seedy breadcrumb mix to coat on all sides and set aside on a tray. Repeat, to coat all the patties. This can be messy, but that's part of the fun! You can cook them all now or freeze some for another day (see Tip).

To cook the fishcakes, heat a drizzle of olive oil in a large frying pan over a medium-high heat, then fry the fishcakes in batches for about 1 minute on each side until golden and crispy. Place on a tray lined with kitchen paper to absorb the excess oil. After each batch, wipe the pan clean with kitchen paper and add another drizzle of olive oil.

For the sweet chilli mayo, mix the mayonnaise with the sweet chilli sauce. Cut the zested lemon into wedges (or cut fresh wedges). Serve the fishcakes with the mayo dip and enjoy with a salad, if desired.

Tip

To freeze the fishcakes, open-freeze on a lined tray before bagging (so they don't stick together) and defrost thoroughly overnight in the fridge before cooking.

Mediterranean Chicken and Butter Beans

SERVES

2

PREP: 15 mins
COOK: 20 mins, *plus resting*

2 large skinless, boneless
   chicken breasts
generous pinch of dried oregano
drizzle of olive oil
salt and freshly ground
   black pepper

For the bean salad

15g pine nuts
1 x 400g tin butter beans,
   drained and rinsed
1 tbsp olive oil
juice and finely grated zest of
   ½ lemon (preferably unwaxed)
½ tsp dried oregano
1 garlic clove, crushed
2 baby cucumbers, diced,
   sliced or roughly chopped
100g baby plum tomatoes,
   halved
¼ red onion, very thinly sliced
25g pitted Kalamata olives,
   sliced
40g feta cheese, crumbled

For the lemon yoghurt drizzle

60g plain (natural) yoghurt
juice and finely grated zest of
   ½ lemon (preferably unwaxed)
1 garlic clove, crushed
¼ tsp dried oregano

This is sunshine and wind on one plate. Sunshine from the delicious chicken and lemony yoghurt dressing, and incoming wind from those gut-healthy butter beans. This is a nutritious lunch: keep eating like this and you are going to start feeling really good, both inside and out.

Preheat the oven to 220°C (200°C fan/gas mark 7) and line a small baking tray with baking paper.

Place the chicken breasts on the lined baking tray and season with a little salt and pepper. Scatter over the dried oregano and drizzle with the olive oil, brushing the seasoning over evenly. Bake in the oven for about 20 minutes, until cooked through, then remove and set aside to rest, covered with foil, for at least 8–10 minutes. Just before serving, cut into 1–1.5cm-thick slices.

Meanwhile, toast the pine nuts. Place them in a dry frying pan over a medium-high heat and toast for 3–4 minutes, until golden, shaking the pan occasionally, then remove from the pan and set aside.

Combine the butter beans, olive oil, lemon juice and zest, oregano, garlic, cucumber, tomatoes, onion, olives and feta in a large bowl. Mix well to combine.

Divide the bean mix between two plates or bowls and top with the sliced, rested chicken.

Make the lemon yoghurt drizzle by whisking together all the ingredients in a small bowl. Drizzle the dressing over the salad and scatter over the toasted pine nuts before enjoying.

Tip

To air-fry the chicken, cook at 200°C for 16–18 minutes (until cooked through), then rest and slice.

Chicken 'Enchilada' Lettuce Bowl

SERVES

2

PREP: 15 mins
COOK: 15 mins, *plus cooling*

For the spicy chicken

2 tbsp double-concentrated
    tomato puree
2 tsp apple cider vinegar
½ tsp ground cumin
½ tsp chilli powder
½ tsp garlic powder
½ dried oregano
1 tbsp olive oil
4–5 skinless, boneless chicken
    thighs (about 450g), cut into
    dice around 1.5cm
salt and freshly ground
    black pepper

For the salad

2 little gem lettuces, trimmed
    and thinly sliced
handful of coriander leaves,
    chopped
1 tbsp olive oil
80g baby plum tomatoes,
    halved
20g pitted black olives, sliced
50g soured cream
30g extra-mature cheddar
    cheese, grated
1 red chilli, thinly sliced
    (deseeded if preferred)
½ lime, cut into wedges,
    to serve

This is the perfect cross between an enchilada and a salad. The spicy chicken seasoned with cumin, chilli, garlic and oregano is paired with a fresh, crunchy salad, and the whole thing tastes out of this world. You can also throw it into a wrap and toast in a pan for a whopper crunchy tortilla wrap. Next time you have a long day out of the house, give this a try and take it with you.

Combine the tomato puree, apple cider vinegar, cumin, chilli powder, garlic powder and dried oregano in a small bowl. Add 1–2 tablespoons of water to loosen it a little, then set aside.

Heat the oil in a large frying pan or wok over a high heat. Add the chicken to the pan, spreading the pieces out evenly, and cook for 9–10 minutes, stirring until the pieces are browned on all sides.

Add the spicy tomato mixture, reduce the heat to medium and simmer for 1–2 minutes, stirring, until the sauce thickens and coats the chicken. Remove from the heat and set aside to cool. Season with a little salt and pepper.

Meanwhile, make the salad. Combine the lettuces and half the chopped coriander in a bowl. Drizzle over the olive oil, season with salt and toss to combine.

Divide the dressed lettuce between two bowls, add the tomatoes, olives and spicy chicken mix. Spoon a dollop of soured cream over each portion and scatter with equal amounts of the cheese, chilli and remaining coriander (or serve the cheese on the side). Serve with the lime wedges to squeeze over.

Enjoy immediately or store the salad in the fridge in an airtight container for up to 2–3 days, keeping the olive oil separately and tossing it with the salad before serving.

Tip

Use slow-cooked chicken (see page 184): shred the meat after slow cooking, add the spicy tomato mix and warm through for 1–2 minutes.

Tip

Air-fry the chicken at 220°C for 16–18 minutes (until cooked), then rest and slice.

Chop the chicken, mix everything and use as a wrap or sandwich filling.

Chicken and Chorizo Mixed Bean Bowl

SERVES

2

PREP: 15 mins
COOK: 20 mins, *plus resting*

2 large skinless, boneless
   chicken breasts
½ tsp smoked paprika
1 tbsp olive oil
60g frozen sweetcorn kernels
1 x 400g tin mixed beans,
   drained and rinsed
60g ready-to-eat (cured)
   chorizo, sliced or diced
80g chargrilled roasted red
   peppers (from a jar), drained
   and thinly sliced
¼ small red onion, thinly sliced
30g soft butterhead lettuce,
   roughly chopped (optional)
salt and freshly ground
   black pepper

For the paprika dressing

2 tbsp olive oil
2 tsp red wine vinegar
1 tsp honey
¼ tsp smoked paprika

**Smoked paprika chicken and chorizo work so well together –
it's the ultimate flavour combo. Tipping in a tin of mixed beans
adds loads of extra fibre and a veggie protein hit, making this
a proper winner any day of the week. You will really feel the
difference in your energy levels when your diet starts to look
more like this.**

Preheat the oven to 220°C (200°C fan/gas mark 7) and line
a small baking tray with baking paper.

Place the chicken on the lined baking tray and season with
a little salt and pepper. Sprinkle over the smoked paprika and
drizzle with the olive oil, brushing the seasoning over evenly.
Bake in the oven for about 20 minutes, until cooked through,
then remove and set aside to rest, covered with foil, for at least
8–10 minutes. Just before serving, cut into 1–1.5cm-thick slices.

While the chicken is resting, cook the corn in a small pan of
boiling water for 3–4 minutes until tender. Drain and rinse
in a sieve under cold running water. Combine the corn,
mixed beans, chorizo, roasted red peppers and red onion in
a large bowl.

Make the dressing by whisking together all the ingredients in
a small bowl. Season with salt and pepper. Drizzle the dressing
over the bean salad, tossing well to combine. Top with the rested
chicken. Serve it as it is, or serve with butterhead lettuce.

Enjoy immediately or store the salad in an airtight container in
the fridge for up to 2–3 days, keeping the dressing separately
and adding it just before serving, to ensure the lettuce doesn't
wilt (if using).

Shredded Chicken with Tabbouleh-style Salad

SERVES

2

PREP: 15 mins
COOK: 20-25 mins, *plus cooling*

50g bulgur wheat, rinsed
40g baby plum tomatoes, finely chopped
1 baby cucumber, diced very small
very generous handful of parsley leaves, finely chopped (about 5 tbsp after finely chopping)
generous handful of coriander leaves, finely chopped (about 3 tbsp after finely chopping)
handful of mint leaves, finely chopped (about 1½ tbsp after finely chopping)
2 tbsp olive oil, plus extra for drizzling
juice of 1 lemon (about 2 tbsp)
200g shredded slow-cooked chicken (see page 184) or succulent, cooked and sliced chicken breasts
salt and freshly ground black pepper

Tabbouleh is one of the freshest and tastiest things you can eat. The mint, parsley and coriander give it so much flavour. This uses the Slow-cooked Shredded Chicken from page 184, but it will also work with cooked chicken breast, if you prefer. This may look like a light chicken salad, but with the extra drizzle of olive oil, it contains plenty of energy.

Cook the bulgur wheat in a saucepan of boiling water for 10–15 minutes, until the bulgur is tender (or according to the packet instructions). Drain, fluff the bulgur with a fork and let it cool.

Combine the cooled bulgur, tomatoes, cucumber and the huge pile of finely chopped herbs in a large bowl. Drizzle over the 2 tablespoons of olive oil and the lemon juice, season with salt and pepper and toss well to combine.

Serve alongside the shredded chicken (or mix the whole lot together), drizzling more olive oil over the chicken. Season the whole lot with more pepper, if needed.

PROTEIN *BOOST*

Add more chicken, with a touch more oil and lemon juice, or add rinsed tinned chickpeas.

Turkey Sandwich with Chipotle Dressing

MAKES

2

large
sandwiches

PREP: 10 mins

4 large slices of sourdough,
  buttered
60g iceberg lettuce, shredded
  or thinly sliced
½ ripe avocado, stoned, peeled
  and diced very small or very
  thinly sliced
50g baby plum tomatoes, sliced
10g sunflower seeds
¼ small red onion, very thinly
  sliced
125g deli-style sliced turkey
  breast (about 6 slices)
salt and freshly ground
  black pepper

**For the creamy chipotle
dressing**

50g crème fraîche
2 tsp chipotle paste

Who doesn't love a sandwich? They're easy, reliable and portable. This one has all the good stuff going on, as well as a spicy chipotle dressing. I use deli-style sliced turkey breast here, but the sando would taste just as delicious with cooked sliced chicken breast instead.

Make the creamy chipotle dressing by combining the crème fraîche and chipotle paste in a small bowl. Season with salt and pepper.

Layer the fillings on 2 slices of the bread, starting with generous dollops of the creamy chipotle dressing, followed by the shredded lettuce, then the avocado, tomatoes, sunflower seeds, red onion and turkey. Season with salt and pepper and top with another slice of bread.

This sandwich is best enjoyed fresh, but if you're prepping ahead, you can wrap it up and keep it in the fridge overnight. Keep in mind that the avocado may lose its freshness after the first day, however.

Tip

Use this delicious combination of ingredients to create easy, grab-and-go, make-ahead wraps (using soft tortillas).

Chimichurri Steak with Rice and Rocket

SERVES

2

PREP: 10 mins
COOK: 15 mins, *plus resting*

2 sirloin steaks, visible fat
    removed
1 tbsp olive oil
pinch of dried oregano
salt and freshly ground
    black pepper

For the chimichurri drizzle

very generous handful of
    parsley leaves (at least 7g),
    finely chopped
1 large garlic clove, crushed
½ tsp dried oregano
½ tsp dried chilli flakes
2 tbsp olive oil
1 tbsp red wine vinegar

For the salad

250g packet of ready-cooked
    basmati rice
2 tbsp olive oil
pinch of dried oregano
60g baby plum tomatoes,
    halved or sliced
40g wild rocket

This is a wonderful recipe – I make it a lot. I can't believe how good home-made chimichurri tastes when it's drizzled over steak. If you don't fancy red meat, you could serve this with grilled chicken breast and it will still taste banging.

Remove the steaks from the fridge about 30 minutes before cooking.

Season the steaks on both sides with salt and pepper, then add the oil to a large frying pan and place over a high heat. Add the steaks and cook for 2 minutes on each side (for medium doneness). Cook for 45–60 seconds longer on each side for thicker cuts, or longer still if you prefer your steaks more well done. Set the steaks aside on a clean chopping board, scatter over the dried oregano, then cover with foil and leave to rest for 8–10 minutes before slicing into 1.5cm-thick pieces.

While the steak rests, make the chimichurri drizzle by combining all the ingredients in a bowl. Season with salt and pepper, if needed.

Empty the ready-cooked rice into a large bowl. Add the olive oil and oregano, then season with salt and pepper. Mix well to combine. Plate the seasoned rice, tomatoes and rocket and top with the sliced steak. Drizzle the chimichurri mix over the salad.

Enjoy immediately or store the salad in an airtight container in the fridge for up to 2–3 days, keeping the dressing separately to ensure the rocket doesn't wilt and adding it just before serving.

Meatballs, Minty Lentils and Feta

SERVES

2

(ensure the meatballs are GF)

PREP: 15 mins
COOK: 20 mins

12 shop-bought beef meatballs
1 tbsp olive oil
235g ready-cooked lentils (drained, if using tinned)
1 baby cucumber, diced, sliced or roughly chopped
50g baby spinach
30g feta cheese, crumbled

For the dressing

2 tbsp olive oil
2 tsp apple cider vinegar
1 garlic clove, crushed
handful of mint leaves, finely chopped, plus extra to serve
salt and freshly ground black pepper

To serve (optional)

2 tbsp plain (natural) yoghurt, preferably Greek yoghurt
30g pomegranate seeds

There's nothing wrong with a cheeky shortcut every now and again. I wish I had time to make everything from scratch, but it's not always possible, and shop-bought meatballs are a simple timesaver. This can be thrown together quickly and you will be left with a really healthy and tasty plate of food. The pomegranate is not essential, but it does add a beautiful sweet crunch alongside the crumbly cheese.

Preheat the oven to 220°C (200°C fan/gas mark 7) and line a baking tray with baking paper.

Spread the meatballs out on the lined tray, drizzle with the olive oil, toss to coat and cook in the oven for 15–18 minutes, until cooked through.

Combine the lentils, cucumber, spinach and feta in a bowl. Divide between two serving bowls or plates and top with the meatballs.

Make the dressing by whisking together all the ingredients in a small bowl, seasoning to taste. Drizzle the dressing over the salad and finish with a spoonful of yoghurt (if using), along with a scattering of pomegranate seeds (if using) and extra mint.

Enjoy immediately or store the salad in the fridge in an airtight container for up to 2–3 days, keeping the dressing separately to ensure the spinach doesn't wilt and adding it just before serving.

Tip

To air-fry the oiled meatballs, cook at 220°C for 12–14 minutes (until cooked through), shaking the basket halfway through cooking.

Overnight Oats for the Win

MAKES

8

servings

PREP: 10 mins, *plus overnight soaking*

For the overnight oats base

440g rolled oats
880ml whole milk
3 tbsp honey
2 tsp vanilla extract

Ever since I came across the term 'overnight oats' I've been obsessed. They taste amazing and can be served in endless flavour and topping combinations, and here are four great ideas for you to try. If you struggle with eating breakfast first thing, this could be a tasty option for a mid-morning work snack or lunch. The oats travel well and will keep in the fridge for a few days.

Combine the oats, milk, honey and vanilla in a large bowl. Cover and leave in the fridge overnight. The next morning, flavour with your chosen additions (see below for ideas).

Store in appropriate serving tubs (with airtight lids for easy transportation) in the fridge for a few days until ready to tuck in.

Strawberry jam and peanut butter

PROTEIN: 18g

To make two little pots of a strawberry jam and peanut butter version, combine 330g of the overnight oats base with 2 tbsp plain (natural) yoghurt, preferably Greek yoghurt. Divide the mix between two appropriate serving tubs, layering each with 1 tbsp strawberry jam and 1 tbsp peanut butter. Top with some chopped peanuts and chopped or sliced strawberries, if you have any at hand.

Lemon and poppy seed

PROTEIN: 14g

To make two little pots of a lemon and poppy seed version, combine 330g of the overnight oats base with 2 tbsp plain (natural) yoghurt, preferably Greek yoghurt. Stir through ½ tsp poppy seeds and the finely grated zest of 1 lemon (preferably unwaxed), along with a squeeze of juice from just ½ the zested lemon. Divide the mix between two appropriate serving tubs, drizzling with more honey if desired.

Apple and flaxseed

PROTEIN: 15g

To make two little pots of an apple and flaxseed version,
combine 330g of the overnight oats base with 2 tbsp plain
(natural) yoghurt, preferably Greek yoghurt. Stir through 2 tsp
ground flaxseed and 1 cored and finely chopped Granny Smith
apple. Divide the mix between two appropriate serving tubs,
drizzling with more honey if desired.

Red berry and mixed seed

PROTEIN: 15g

To make two little pots of a red berry and mixed seed version,
combine 330g of the overnight oats base with 2 tbsp plain
(natural) yoghurt, preferably Greek yoghurt. Stir through 100g
fresh mixed berries (raspberries and strawberries; larger ones
chopped smaller). Divide the mix between two appropriate
serving tubs, drizzling with more honey if desired, then
scatter over 1 tsp toasted mixed seeds (see toasting method
on page 145).

FAST-PREP, SLOW-COOK BANGERS

Slow-cooked Shredded Chicken

MAKES

1

large batch

PREP: 5 mins
COOK: 1½ hours, *plus resting*

1kg skinless, boneless chicken
   breasts
400ml chicken stock (made
   with 1 stock cube)
1 tsp dried oregano
1 tsp garlic powder
1 tsp ground paprika
salt and freshly ground
   black pepper

I'm embarrassingly late to the party with slow cooking, but honestly, it's a game changer, especially for cooking proteins, and I love using my slow cooker! This recipe takes chicken breasts – which can often be pretty dry and boring – and makes them moreish, with a texture that is so tender and juicy. They become super versatile and are perfect for adding to pastas, soups or wraps. If you haven't got a slow cooker, you can cook it low and slow on a hob instead, no problem.

Put the chicken breasts in a large, deep pan, add the chicken stock, oregano, garlic powder and paprika. Bring to a gentle simmer over a medium heat, then cover with a well-fitting lid and reduce the heat to low. Cook for 1½ hours until the chicken is tender and easy to shred.

When done, use tongs to carefully remove the breasts and place them in a large bowl. Cover with foil and leave to rest for 15–20 minutes. Reserve 100ml of the cooking stock.

After resting, use two forks to shred the meat. Add the reserved cooking stock and mix in. Lightly season with salt and pepper, then set aside, or portion and refrigerate (or freeze).

FOR THE SLOW COOKER: Put the chicken breasts in the slow cooker, add the chicken stock, oregano, garlic powder and paprika, cover and cook on low for 5–6 hours. When done, use tongs to remove the breasts and place them in a large bowl. Cover with foil and leave to rest for 15–20 minutes. Reserve 100ml of the cooking stock. Shred the meat as above, adding the reserved stock, and portion and store.

Slow-cooked Beef Mince and Lentils

MAKES

1

large batch

PREP: 5 mins
COOK: 3½ hours

1.2kg 5%-fat minced beef
200g uncooked green lentils
900ml beef stock (made with
   2 stock cubes)
2 tsp dried oregano
salt and freshly ground
   black pepper

This simple, delicious beef and lentil mix is perfect for high-protein batch cooking. It can be made over a gentle heat on the hob or in a slow cooker, and works perfectly on rice, with pasta, in wraps or in tacos. I can't think of anything better than walking in the door to the smell of slow-cooked meat doing its thing.

Place the mince and lentils into a large, deep pan. Add the beef stock and oregano, bring to a gentle simmer over a medium heat, then cover with a well-fitting lid and reduce the heat to low.

Cook for 3½ hours. Remove the lid in the final 45–60 minutes to help the mixture reduce. This lets any excess liquid evaporate, giving it a thick, rich consistency that's ready to portion up. Season with salt and pepper, then set aside, or portion and refrigerate (or freeze) as needed.

FOR THE SLOW COOKER: Place the mince and lentils into the slow cooker. Add the beef stock and oregano, then cover and cook on low for 5–6 hours. Remove the lid of the slow cooker in the final 45–60 minutes to help the mixture reduce. This lets any excess liquid evaporate, giving it a thick, rich consistency that's ready to portion up. Season, portion and refrigerate (or freeze).

Unbelievable Chicken and Cashew Nut Stew

SERVES

4

PREP: 15 mins
COOK: 2½ hours

150g unsalted cashew nuts

2 tbsp olive oil, plus extra for drizzling

1 onion, roughly chopped

2 garlic cloves, peeled and halved

1 tbsp double-concentrated tomato puree

2 tsp garam masala

1 tsp salt

1 tsp chilli powder

¼ tsp turmeric

1 lemon, halved

800g skinless, boneless chicken thighs, cut into bite-size chunks

200g chestnut mushrooms, quartered

350ml chicken stock (made with 1 stock cube)

85g dried apricots, finely chopped (or raisins)

100g creamed coconut block, roughly chopped

2 tsp honey

salt and ground black pepper

To serve

280g uncooked rice (any kind)

4 (heaped) tbsp Greek yoghurt

drizzle of sweet chilli sauce

handful of coriander leaves

This tastes unbelievably good. It's warm, comforting, rich, sweet and a little spicy, and the yoghurty drizzle just caps it off so well. Come on. Look at it. It's beautiful.

Preheat the oven to 190°C (170°C fan/gas mark 5) and line a baking tray with baking paper. Spread the cashew nuts out on the tray and toast in the oven for 6–8 minutes.

Put 85g of the cashew nuts in a food processor and roughly chop the rest, setting aside for now. Add the 2 tablespoons of olive oil, onion, garlic, tomato puree, garam masala, salt, chilli powder, turmeric and the juice of 1 lemon half to the food processor and blitz until smooth(ish), scraping down the bowl between blitzing, to make the curry paste.

Now brown the chicken in batches. Heat a drizzle of olive oil in a large, deep pan over a high heat, add some chicken and cook for 4–5 minutes until golden brown on all sides. Remove from the pan using a slotted spoon, set aside in a bowl, and brown the remaining chicken in the same way, adding more oil, if needed. Add another drizzle of oil, then add the mushrooms and cook over a high heat for 1–2 minutes, stirring, until they start to caramelise. Add the stock and prepared curry paste and reduce over a medium heat for about 1 minute. Return the chicken to the pan, add the apricots (or raisins), mix well, then cover and cook over a low to medium-low heat for 2 hours.

Use a slotted spoon to remove the chicken and mushrooms and place into a large bowl. Increase the heat to medium-high and crumble in the creamed coconut pieces, whisking to dissolve. Cook for 7–8 minutes until the sauce thickens. Stir in the honey and season with salt and pepper. Once the sauce is very thick, pour it over the strained chicken mix. Stir in the remaining chopped cashew nuts.

Meanwhile, cook the rice according to the packet instructions. Season with salt and pepper.

Serve the fragrant chicken with the rice and yoghurt. Drizzle with the sweet chilli sauce and finish with the coriander.

Tip

To toast the cashew nuts in an air fryer, cook at 190°C for 5–6 minutes until golden, shaking the basket halfway through.

Chipotle Chicken (Riced or Wrapped)

SERVES

4–6

PREP: 10 mins
COOK: 20 mins, *not including the slow-cooked chicken*

2 tbsp olive oil
1 onion, finely chopped
1 red pepper, deseeded and finely diced
2 garlic cloves, crushed
½ tsp dried oregano
200g passata
200ml chicken stock (made with ½ stock cube)
1 tbsp double-concentrated tomato puree
1 tsp honey
3 tbsp chipotle paste
400g shredded slow-cooked chicken (see page 184), or use succulent, cooked and thinly sliced chicken breasts

Time-saver alert. If you've made a big batch of the Slow-cooked Shredded Chicken (page 184), this is an awesome one to make today. The spicy chipotle sauce brings the shredded chicken to life and works so well served with rice or thrown into a wrap and turned into a burrito.

Option 1: Serve with rice
(serves 4)

PROTEIN: 32g

280g uncooked wild rice or white rice (or mix of both)
salt
4 tbsp reduced-fat soured cream
1 small ripe avocado, stoned, peeled and thinly sliced (optional)
small handful of coriander leaves, chopped
1 lime, cut into wedges, to serve

Option 2: Wrap it up!
(makes 6 wraps – one per serving)

PROTEIN: 19g

6 soft high-protein tortillas
juice of 1 lime (about 2 tsp)
1 small ripe avocado, stoned, peeled and thinly sliced
4 tsp reduced-fat soured cream
handful of coriander leaves, chopped

PROTEIN BOOST

Serve with Black Bean and Mixed Veg Salad (page 145).

Heat the oil in a large frying pan over a medium heat, add the onion and red pepper and cook for 6–7 minutes until softened and starting to caramelise. Stir in the garlic and oregano and cook for another minute until fragrant. Add the passata, stock, tomato puree and honey, reduce the heat to medium and simmer for 3–4 minutes until thickened. Add the chipotle paste and all the shredded, cooked chicken and mix well to evenly combine and warm the chicken through.

If serving with rice, cook the rice according to the packet instructions (usually in a saucepan of boiling water for 10–15 minutes: wild rice may take 3–4 minutes longer). Once cooked, drain the rice in a sieve and season with salt. Serve the chipotle chicken with the rice and spoon over a dollop of soured cream over each portion. Add the avocado (if using), scatter with coriander and serve with a lime wedge.

If making wraps, divide the chipotle chicken evenly among the soft tortillas. Squeeze a little lime juice over each and top with equal amounts of the sliced avocado, a dollop of the soured cream and a scattering of the coriander. Fold in the sides of the tortilla, then roll tightly from the bottom up. If keeping some for the next day, wrap tightly in foil and store in the fridge.

Chicken and Red Lentil Soup

SERVES

4

PREP: 15 mins
COOK: 1¾ hours

1 tbsp olive oil
1 onion, finely chopped
1 carrot, peeled and finely chopped
2 garlic cloves, crushed
1 tsp ground cumin
1 tsp ground paprika
½ tsp dried mixed herbs
1 green cardamom pod, lightly bruised
1 litre chicken stock (made with 2 stock cubes)
1 x 400g tin chopped tomatoes
4 large skinless, boneless chicken breasts, or 8 large skinless, boneless chicken thighs (about 800g), sliced
120g dried red lentils, rinsed
70g baby spinach
80g feta cheese, crumbled
salt and freshly ground black pepper
1 lemon, cut into wedges, to serve

You will love the taste of this warm, comforting and satisfying soup. I make it a lot during the colder months; it's perfect to have in the fridge, ready to reheat after a long day, warm yourself up and help you get to bed nice and early. A proper bowlful of goodness here and one you'll be thinking about the next day, wishing you had more left over.

Heat the oil in a large, deep saucepan over a medium heat, add the onion and carrot and cook for 5–6 minutes until starting to caramelise. Add the garlic, spices, mixed herbs and cardamom pod, stir well to combine, then add the stock and tomatoes and bring to the boil. Reduce the heat to medium-low, add the chicken and lentils and mix well. Cover and cook for 1 hour.

Remove the chicken pieces with tongs and place them in a bowl, then continue cooking the soup for 30 minutes, while the chicken rests, covered with foil. Once rested, use two forks to roughly shred the meat.

Pick out and discard the cardamom pod from the soup and add the spinach, mixing well to wilt it. Season to taste.

Divide the shredded chicken among four warm soup bowls and ladle in the lentil soup. Top with the crumbled feta and serve with the lemon wedges to squeeze over before slurping up!

FOR THE SLOW COOKER: Follow step 1 above. Once everything in the pan is simmering, transfer to the slow cooker and add the chicken and lentils. Cover and cook for 6 hours on low. In the last 30 minutes, remove the chicken pieces with tongs and place them in a bowl. Cover with foil, rest, then shred, as above.

Pick out and discard the cardamom pod, turn off the slow cooker and stir in the spinach. Taste the soup and adjust the seasoning with salt and pepper. Serve in warm soup bowls as above.

Tip

This soup keeps well in an airtight container in the fridge for up to 3 days and freezes well, too. Just leave the feta and lemon out until you're ready to serve.

Pulled Pork with Mustard Yoghurt Slaw

SERVES

4

PREP: 15 mins
COOK: 2–3 hours, *plus resting*

For the pulled pork

600g thick pork shoulder steaks
    or pork loin steaks
200g passata
1 tbsp Worcestershire sauce
1 tsp smoked paprika
1 tsp garlic powder
½ tsp dried chilli flakes
100g BBQ sauce
salt and freshly ground
    black pepper

For the mustard slaw

100g plain (natural) yoghurt,
    preferably Greek yoghurt
2 tbsp apple cider vinegar
1 tbsp wholegrain mustard
1 tsp honey
2 garlic cloves, crushed
100g savoy cabbage, shredded
    or thinly sliced
1 medium carrot, peeled and
    grated
¼ red onion, very thinly sliced

To serve (optional)

4 seeded buns, buttered

Slow-cooked pork is one of the most delicious things around. The way the low temperature breaks down the proteins and makes the meat beyond tender keeps me coming back to this recipe at least once a month. The sweet and smoky BBQ sauce and home-made mustard slaw combo here is quite literally da bomb! The person who invented the slow cooker must have had pork in mind, so I've included a method in case you have one.

Put the pork steaks in a large, deep saucepan and add the passata, Worcestershire sauce, smoked paprika, garlic powder and chilli flakes. Bring to a gentle simmer over a medium heat, then cover with a well-fitting lid and reduce the heat to low. Cook for 2–3 hours until the pork is tender and easy to shred. Use tongs to carefully transfer the pork into a large bowl. Cover with foil and rest for 20 minutes.

Cook the remaining sauce in the pan for 3–6 minutes over a high heat until reduced by half, adding the BBQ sauce in the last 1–2 minutes. Once thickened, remove the pan from the heat.

Once the pork has rested, use two forks to shred the meat. Add the sauce and set aside.

Meanwhile, make the slaw. Mix the yoghurt, vinegar, mustard, honey and garlic in a large bowl and season with salt and pepper. Add the cabbage, carrot and onion and toss well to coat and combine.

Serve the pulled pork with the slaw, or make sandwiches using seeded buns, filling them with the pulled pork topped generously with the slaw.

FOR THE SLOW COOKER: Put the pork steaks in a slow cooker and add the passata, Worcestershire sauce, smoked paprika, garlic powder and chilli flakes. Cover with the lid and cook on low for 6 hours. Once done, use tongs to carefully transfer the pork into a large bowl. Cover and rest for 20 minutes. Transfer all the juices from the slow cooker into a large saucepan and cook for 3–6 minutes over a high heat until reduced by half, adding the BBQ sauce in the last 1–2 minutes. Once thickened, remove the pan from the heat.

Shred the meat and add the sauce, as above, then make the slaw and serve.

Joe's OG Chicken Pie

SERVES

4

PREP: 15 mins
COOK: 45 mins

2–4 tbsp olive oil, plus extra for brushing

800g shredded slow-cooked chicken (see page 184) or 7–8 skinless, boneless chicken thighs, chopped into bite-size chunks

2 large leeks, trimmed and thinly sliced

250g chestnut mushrooms, sliced

3 garlic cloves, crushed

5–6 thyme sprigs, leaves picked

60ml dry white wine

100g soured cream

3–4 sheets of filo pastry (about 90g total)

2 tsp white sesame seeds

salt and freshly ground black pepper

You may remember a true classic called 'Joe's chicken pie' from my first cookbook, *Lean in 15*. Fast forward ten years, and I decided to tweak that original recipe, ending up with this new and improved version. I've added dry white wine, fresh thyme, soured cream and some sesame seeds, all of which take the OG to a new level of flavour and joy. I hope this becomes a firm favourite in your home, too.

Preheat the oven to 190°C (170°C fan/gas mark 5) and have a medium, deep baking/roasting dish (like a lasagne dish) ready.

If you are cooking the chicken from scratch, heat some oil in a large frying pan or wok over a high heat, add half the chicken pieces and cook for 4–5 minutes until golden brown on all sides (there's no need to cook them through at this stage). Remove from the pan and set aside in a bowl, then brown the rest of the chicken in the same way, adding more oil, if needed. Season with salt and pepper and set aside.

Add a little more oil to the same pan, turn the heat down to medium, add the leeks and mushrooms and cook for 3–5 minutes, stirring, until softened and starting to caramelise. Add the garlic and thyme and cook for another minute, stirring regularly to prevent the garlic burning. Add the white wine and turn the heat up to medium-high. The wine will deglaze the pan, so continue to cook and scrape the bottom of the pan with a wooden spoon, until all the super-tasty bits that may have stuck to the pan are loosened.

Return the chicken to the pan (along with any juices from the bowl) – or add the cooked shredded chicken – and mix well to combine. Turn the heat down to low and stir in the soured cream. Season with salt and pepper and simmer gently for 4–5 minutes to thicken while you prepare the filo.

Lay the sheets of filo out on a clean work surface and brush each sheet lightly with olive oil using a pastry brush.

Tip the thickened chicken and mushroom mix into the baking dish. Lightly crunch up each piece of oiled filo pastry and place them on top of the mixture. Scatter over the sesame seeds and bake in the oven for 15–20 minutes, or until the pastry is golden and crisp.

Tip

Gluten-free? No problem! Top it with a layer of mash instead (see page 70) and you're sorted.

Low and Slow Mince with Veg and Rice

SERVES

4

mince only,
not the rice

PREP: 10 mins
COOK: 25 mins *(not including the slow-cooked beef and lentils)*

For the roasted veg and rice

1 red pepper, deseeded and
  roughly chopped
1 courgette, roughly chopped
½ red onion, cut into wedges
1 tsp dried oregano
2 tbsp olive oil
200g uncooked wild rice or
  white rice (or a mix of both)
generous handful of flat-leaf
  parsley leaves, chopped
salt and freshly ground
  black pepper
1 lemon, cut into wedges,
  to serve

For the mince

½ batch slow-cooked beef
  mince and lentils (see page
  185)
1 tbsp double-concentrated
  tomato puree
1 tsp dried oregano
juice and finely grated zest
  of 2 lemons (preferably
  unwaxed)

This is a cracking way to turn your batch-cooked beef and lentil mince into a wonderfully fresh and nutritious meal any night of the week. It has lots of healthy roasted veg alongside a mountain of rice and it contains all the ingredients for a perfect family meal.

Preheat the oven to 200°C (180°C fan/gas mark 6) and line a large baking tray with baking paper.

Put the red pepper, courgette and red onion wedges in a large bowl with the dried oregano and olive oil. Season with salt and pepper and toss to coat. Spread out on the lined baking tray and roast in the oven for 20–22 minutes until the vegetables are tender and starting to caramelise.

Meanwhile, cook the rice according to the packet instructions (usually in a saucepan of boiling water for 10–15 minutes: wild rice may take 3–4 minutes longer). Once cooked, drain the rice in a sieve and season with salt.

Stir all the roasted vegetables and half the chopped parsley into the cooked rice. Set aside to keep warm.

Warm through the slow-cooked beef mince and lentils in a large frying pan over a medium heat, then add the tomato puree, oregano and lemon juice and zest, adding a splash of water if needed. Cook gently for a few minutes until thick, chunky and delicious. Season with salt and generously with cracks of black pepper.

Serve the mince with the rice and scatter over the remaining parsley. Enjoy with the lemon wedges on the side to squeeze over.

PROTEIN *BOOST*

Replace the rice with quinoa (see page 154 for how to do this).

Tip

Make tortilla wraps with the leftovers for lunch, adding gem lettuce, grated cheese, avocado, soured cream, a squeeze of lime, chilli and herbs if you fancy.

Mexican-style Beef Stew with Rice

SERVES

4

PREP: 15 mins
COOK: 3–4 hours

2–3 tbsp olive oil
1 onion, finely chopped
1 green pepper, deseeded
and finely diced
200g chestnut mushrooms,
finely chopped
3 garlic cloves, crushed
2 tbsp ground cumin
2 tsp ground coriander
1–2 tsp cayenne pepper,
to taste
100ml red wine
1 x 400g tin chopped tomatoes
200ml beef stock (made with
½ stock cube)
800g beef stewing chunks
1 x 400g tin kidney beans,
drained and rinsed
salt and black pepper

To serve

4 x 125g packets ready-cooked
basmati rice, heated
40g extra-mature cheddar
cheese, grated
4 heaped tbsp soured cream
2 avocados, stoned and sliced
1 red chilli, thinly sliced
handful of parsley or coriander
(or mix of both), chopped
1 lime, cut into wedges

Slow-cooked chunks of beef in a marvellous Mexican-style sauce with rice? This sounds like a dream – the ultimate family meal. Everyone will be leaving the dinner table with a smile and a full belly after this. I love the freshness of the avocado, fresh parsley and soured cream on top. Perfect!

Heat 2 tablespoons of the oil in a large, deep saucepan over a medium-high heat, add the onion and green pepper and cook for 3–4 minutes until starting to soften and caramelise. Add the mushrooms (and more oil, if needed) and cook for another 2–3 minutes, stirring until the mushrooms start to caramelise. Add the garlic and spices and cook, stirring, for about 1 minute. Pour in the wine, increase the heat to high and simmer for 1–2 minutes until the wine has completely evaporated. Add the tomatoes and beef stock to the pan, bring to a simmer, then add the beef. Cover, reduce the heat to low and cook for 3–3½ hours until the beef is tender. When there is 1 hour remaining, add the kidney beans and uncover to ensure the mixture thickens. Season to taste.

Serve with the rice and top with the grated cheese, soured cream, sliced avocados, red chilli, herbs and lime wedges to squeeze over.

FOR THE SLOW COOKER: Tip the beef into the slow cooker (don't turn it on yet). Follow the method above, cooking the vegetables in a large frying pan or saucepan, before adding the spices, followed by the wine, tomatoes and stock. Stir, then transfer to the slow cooker, stirring it into the beef. Cover and turn the slow cooker to low. Cook for 6 hours, stirring in the kidney beans and removing the lid of the slow cooker in the last hour, to ensure the mixture thickens. Season to taste and serve as above.

/ FAST-PREP, SLOW-COOK BANGERS

Lamb and Chickpea Tagine

SERVES

4

PREP: 15 mins
COOK: 3½–4 hours

1 tbsp olive oil
1 onion, finely chopped
2 garlic cloves, crushed
1 tsp ground ginger
1 tsp ground cumin
1 tsp ground coriander
2 tsp ground cinnamon
½ tsp turmeric
½ tsp dried chilli flakes
600g diced lean lamb leg or
    shoulder
1 x 400g tin chickpeas, drained
    and rinsed
2 tbsp double-concentrated
    tomato puree
1 x 400g tin chopped tomatoes
1 tbsp honey
80g dried apricots, finely
    chopped (or raisins)
salt and freshly ground
    black pepper

For the nutty quinoa

450ml chicken stock (made
    with 1 stock cube)
200g quinoa
60g toasted pine nuts
finely grated zest of 1 lemon
    (preferably unwaxed)
handful of coriander leaves,
    chopped, plus extra to serve

This is a special one for when you have a bit more time on your hands. The prep time is short, but what ends up on your plate a few hours later is well and truly worth the wait. The whole house will smell delicious with the aromas of garlic, ginger, cinnamon, apricots and much more. I can't stress enough how good this one tastes, so I hope you get to enjoy it.

Heat the oil in a large, deep saucepan over a medium heat, add the onion and cook for 3–4 minutes until soft and translucent. Stir in the garlic and spices, season with pepper, then add the lamb, chickpeas, tomato puree and chopped tomatoes. Fill the empty tomato tin a third full with water, swirl it around and add this water to the pan. Mix and bring to a gentle simmer over a medium heat. Cover, reduce the heat to low and cook for 3½ hours until the lamb is tender. In the last hour, stir in the honey and apricots (remove the lid if you like, for the mixture to thicken).

To cook the quinoa, bring the stock to the boil in a saucepan. Add the quinoa, reduce the heat to medium, cover partially and simmer for 12–15 minutes until the water is absorbed. The quinoa is cooked when the grains are translucent and the outer germ separates. Fluff with a fork and stir through the pine nuts and lemon zest. Slice the zested lemon and set aside.

Divide the quinoa among four warm bowls and ladle over the lamb. Garnish with the chopped coriander and serve the lemon slices alongside.

FOR THE SLOW COOKER: Cook the onion, garlic, spices, lamb, chickpeas, tomato puree and chopped tomatoes as above, in a large frying pan over a medium heat, swirling water in the tin and adding it too. Bring to a gentle simmer and transfer to the slow cooker. Cover and cook for 6 hours on low. Remove the lid in the last hour so the mixture thickens. In the last 15–20 minutes, add the honey and apricots.

Lovely Lamb and Lentil Curry with Rice

SERVES

4

curry only,
not the rice

**PREP: 15 mins
COOK: 3½–4 hours**

50g creamed coconut block,
   roughly chopped
1 tbsp olive oil
1 onion, finely chopped
2 garlic cloves, crushed
20g fresh ginger, finely grated
1 tsp ground cumin
1 tsp ground coriander
1 tsp garam masala
½ tsp turmeric
½ tsp chilli powder
1 x 400g tin chopped tomatoes
2 tbsp double-concentrated
   tomato puree
450ml beef stock (made with
   1 stock cube)
800g diced lean lamb shoulder
   or leg
100g dried lentils (brown or
   green), rinsed
30g almond butter
salt and freshly ground
   black pepper
generous handful of coriander,
   chopped, to serve

For the almond butter rice

280g uncooked long-grain rice
20g almond butter

Save the best till last. This is one of the top recipes in this whole book for me, and look how excited Indie is to get stuck into it! Slow-cooked lamb is really something special, even on its own. And adding almond butter to fluffy rice is an absolute game changer. It honestly adds this wonderful nutty, creamy texture (and protein, of course), which will make you think... Why have I never thought of that before? Please don't skip this one. It could be your favourite recipe, too.

Whisk the creamed coconut pieces in 200ml boiling-hot water in a heatproof jug until dissolved.

Heat the oil in a large, deep saucepan over a medium heat, add the onion and cook for 3–4 minutes until soft and translucent. Stir in the garlic and ginger and cook for another minute until fragrant, then add the spices, followed by the tomatoes, tomato puree, beef stock and prepared coconut milk. Add the diced lamb and lentils, mix well and bring to a gentle simmer. Cover, reduce the heat to low and cook for 3½ hours until the lamb is tender. In the final 30 minutes, stir in the almond butter. Remove the lid if you want the mixture to thicken.

Towards the end of cooking, cook the rice according to the packet instructions (usually in a saucepan of boiling water for 10–15 minutes). Drain and transfer to a large bowl. Season and stir in the almond butter until the rice is evenly coated. Serve with the rice, scattering over the coriander.

FOR THE SLOW COOKER: Cook the onion, garlic and ginger, spices, tomatoes, tomato puree and beef stock as above. Simmer, transfer to the slow cooker, then add the lamb and lentils.

Dissolve the coconut as above, then add it to the cooker, mix, cover and cook for 6 hours on low. Remove the lid for the last hour to thicken. In the final 30 minutes, stir in the almond butter.

PROTEIN IM 15

JOE WICKS The body COACH

Index

C

Acknowledgements

Creating a cookbook is a proper team effort. I'd like to start by saying a big thank you to Carole Tonkinson, my publisher, for giving me the opportunity to share another book with the world. Thank you to everyone at LEAP (Bonnier Books) who has helped get this awesome book over the line and out in the shops. And thank you to Max Robinson, Laura Nickoll, Lucy Tirahan and Maeve Bargman for all your help and guidance. Thanks too to nutritionist Clare Gray, who calculated all the protein content for me.

A big shout-out to Monya Kilian Palmer for helping me develop and test the incredible recipes. I couldn't have done it without you. Thank you, too, to Mike English for the fantastic food photography and Maeve for her creative direction. I love the photos so much. Also, a big thank you to Kate Wesson for the unreal food styling skills. Kate, you've made everything look so tasty and beautiful.

Finally, thanks to my brother and manager Nikki Wicks for getting the book deal organised and set up. You always believe in me and get the best out of me. Finally, thank you to Rosie, Indie, Marley, Leni and Dusty: the foundation of all my happiness.

Love you all lots.

Joe x

'REAL FOOD *is* **THE BEST** SOURCE OF PROTEIN'

'START SEEING **HEALTHY FOOD** *as* THE **TREAT,** AND **PROTEIN** *as* THE **REWARD'**

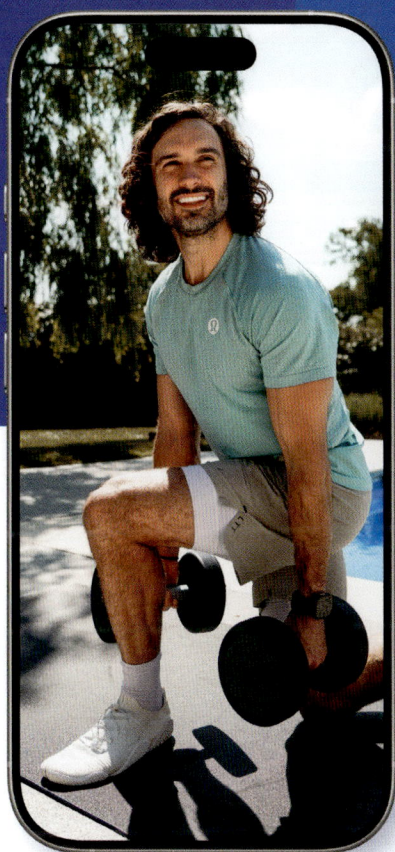

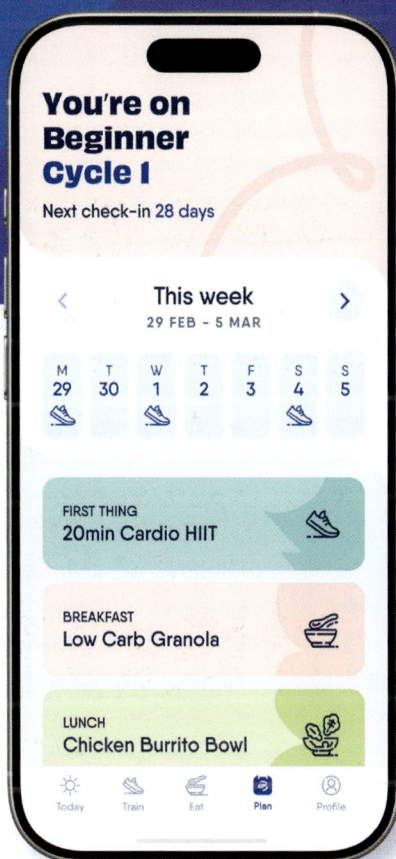

First published in the UK in 2025 by LEAP
An imprint of Bonnier Books UK
5th Floor, HYLO, 105 Bunhill Row,
London, EC1Y 8LZ

A CIP catalogue record for this book is available from the British Library.
Hardback ISBN: 9781785128547
Also available as an ebook

3 5 7 9 10 8 6 4 2

Publisher Carole Tonkinson
Project Manager and Editor Laura Nickoll
Designer and Art Director Maeve Bargman
Photography Mike English Photography
Food Stylist Kate Wesson
Prop Stylist Max Robinson
Printed and bound by Mohn

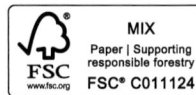

FSC
www.fsc.org

MIX
Paper | Supporting
responsible forestry
FSC® C011124

The authorised representative in the EEA is
Bonnier Books UK (Ireland) Limited.
Registered office address:
Block B, The Crescent Building
Northwood, Santry
Dublin 9, D09 C6X8
Ireland
compliance@bonnierbooks.ie